THE ADEPT INITIATE'S GUIDE TO LUXOR TEMPLE

Symbolism is all around us. Modern symbols, such as icons and logos, convey enough information to fill several thick books. Ancient symbols, similarly, did the same for those who created them. Schwaller de Lubicz spent 15 years studying the Luxor Temple in an effort to decode its symbols and accomplished monumental works. John Anthony West continued his legacy with *Serpent in the Sky* and inspiring the production of a seminal video series called "Ancient Egypt Mystery Schools."

While my focus has mostly been on engineering, I have traveled through Egypt with John Anthony West (2006) and Anyextee (2021) and can say without equivocation that both experiences were immensely valuable to me. Both West and Anyextee were excellent company. Continuing the legacy of de Lubicz and West, Anyextee injects a youthful passion while respecting both conventional and alternative views on history.

> *-Christopher Dunn, author of The Giza Power Plant*
> *and Lost Technologies of Ancient Egypt*

As John West inherited and further developed the work of Schwaller de Lubicz in the study of Egyptian symbology, Anyextee inherited the knowledge of his mentor John West. The more we explore and unearth the hidden secrets of Egypt in this day and age, the more we need scholars and tour leaders like Anyextee continue to lead us to the Next (Anyextee) level.

> *-Normandi Ellis, author of Awakening Osiris*

Anyextee's extensive research, knowledge and esoteric understanding makes this the ultimate guide to the breathtaking Temple of Man. A mesmerising book that takes the reader on a personal journey of discovery.

-*Matt Sibson, Ancient Architects*

For me, The Adept Initiate's Guide to the Luxor Temple follows capably in the footsteps of John Anthony West's The Traveler's Key to Ancient Egypt, with its scope keenly focused on this one important Egyptian site. Anyextee has succeeded in taking a comprehensive view of his subject, making the material very readable for laymen while also bringing more subtle, esoteric aspects of the temple design, structure, and symbolism to the attention of more experienced readers. If you can't join Anyextee himself on your tour of the temple, this book surely is the next best thing.

- *Laird Scranton, author of Primal Wisdom of the Ancients and Sacred Symbols of the Dogon*

This is a brilliant book. Anyone interested in visiting the Luxor Temple in Egypt will find the information in this book essential—even if you are visiting from the comfort of your living room! You will not only get the foundational information about the temple, but you will get enormous amounts of insight, as well as practical spiritual applications, you will not find anywhere else. Anyextee is an "on the ground" expert, which means he spends most of his time wandering the sands of Egypt taking in and investigating the mysteries he so deftly writes about. You will not find this amazing insight anywhere else.

- *Todd Hayden, PhD, author of Ancient Egypt and Modern Psychotherapy: Sacred Science and the Search for Soul*

In *The Adept Initiate's Guide to Luxor Temple*, researcher/explorer/guide Anyextee brings to life the magic, insights and sublime perceptions of the Egyptian Mystery School, in many ways reflecting and emulating the research of John Anthony West, his mentor, and R.A. Schwaller de Lubicz before him. West's work was seminal, and Anyextee is his heir apparent.

-Glenn Kreisberg, author of Spirits in Stone:
The Secrets of Megalithic America

The late, great John Anthony West was responsible for introducing the Symbolist interpretation of ancient Egypt to the world, and now that torch has passed. In his eye-opening new book, Anyextee draws back the veil on the esoteric mysteries of the Temple of Luxor, adeptly expanding on R.A. Schwaller de Lubicz's original, paradigm-shattering insights and guiding his readers on a journey of self-initiation and transformation in the time-tested tradition of the ancient Egyptian sages themselves. Highly recommended.

-Ian Driscoll, author of Atlantis: Egyptian Genesis

Schwaller de Lubicz would create a massive two volume work entitled 'The Temple of Man' which focused on the symbolic and esoteric nature of the Luxor Temple. Having read it many years ago, l can vouch that it is not a light read, and can often be described as heavy going. Anyextee has done an admirable job in condensing this massive opus into a more readable layman's guide, along with further insights from his own study of the temple and that of his mentor John Anthony West. Anyextee's 'The Adept Initiates Guide to Luxor Temple' is a perfect sized guide, which the visitor can easily carry as they explore the temple and its many fascinating features.

-Keith Hamilton, author of A Layman's Guide series

THE **ADEPT INITIATE'S** GUIDE TO **LUXOR TEMPLE**

EXPERIENCING THE
TEMPLE OF MAN
USING THE ESOTERIC
SYMBOLIST APPROACH

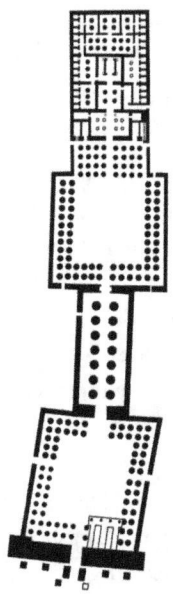

ANYEXTEE

UNUSUAL ACCOMPLISHMENT, LLC DBA ADEPT INITIATES
1380 EAST AVE STE # 124-234
CHICO, CA 95926-7349
adeptinitiates.com

Published by Adept Initiates
Copyright © 2024 Anyextee

ISBN: 979-8-9885682-0-9
LCCN: 2023916308

Cover Design & Illustration: Adrian Baxter
Interior Layout & Graphics: Ken Lawrence
Photographs of Luxor Temple: Anyextee

Publisher's Cataloging-in-Publication Data:
Names: Anyextee, author.
Title: The Adept Initiate's guide to Luxor Temple : experiencing the Temple of Man Using the esoteric symbolist approach / Anyextee.
Description: [First edition]. | [Chico, California] : [Adept Initiates], [2023] | Includes bibliographical references and index.
Identifiers: ISBN: 979-8-9885682-0-9 (paperback) | 979-8-9885682-1-6 (ebook) | LCCN: 2023916308
Subjects: LCSH: Temple of Luxor (Luxor, Egypt)--Symbolic aspects. | Occultism--Egypt. | Symbolism-- Egypt--Luxor. | Signs and symbols--Egypt--Luxor. | Relief (Sculpture)-- Egypt--Luxor-- Symbolic aspects. | Inscriptions, Egyptian--Egypt--Luxor--Symbolic aspects. | Luxor (Egypt)-- Antiquities--Symbolic aspects. | Egypt--Antiquities--Symbolic aspects.
Classification: LCC: BF1434.E3 A59 2023 | DDC: 001.9--dc23

To send correspondence to the author , please use the contact form at anyextee.com

CONTENTS

FIGURES & ILLUSTRATIONS

FOREWORD

by Sayed Mostafa, Egyptologist & Inspectorate of Luxor Temple

In the heart of ancient Thebes, now modern Luxor, lies a monument that has stood the test of time, whispering the secrets of a civilization that has long fascinated the world. Luxor Temple, a testament to human ingenuity and divine aspiration, has been the subject of countless studies, each attempting to unravel its mysteries. It is within this context of perpetual discovery and wonder that Anyextee's book, "The Adept Initiate's Guide to Luxor Temple: Experiencing The Temple of Man Using The Esoteric Symbolist Approach," emerges as a beacon of insight and enlightenment.

Having had the privilege of serving as an Egyptologist and the Inspectorate of Luxor Temple for seven years, I have walked its sacred grounds countless times, each visit revealing a layer unseen, a story untold. The temple is not merely a structure of stone; it is a narrative in itself, a narrative that Anyextee skillfully decodes and presents through a unique lens in this guide.

My walking tour with Anyextee through the temple was not just an exploration of its physical dimensions but a voyage through its spiritual essence. His approach to understanding Luxor Temple transcends the conventional, marrying the scientific with the esoteric, and offering a perspective that is as informative as it is eye-opening. This book is not merely a guide; it is an invitation to journey through Luxor Temple in a way that has seldom been offered before.

Despite lacking formal academic training, Anyextee's dedication to the discipline of Egyptology is heartfelt and profound. As a self-educated, independent researcher proficient in primary sources and skilled in Middle Egyptian hieroglyphics, Anyextee stands among the most authoritative voices in the field.

In a manner reminiscent of Schwaller de Lubicz, Anyextee lived in Luxor, deeply immersed in our local culture as he studied the temple day by day, stone by stone. As a devoted student of the symbolist school - which, though initially not accepted by orthodox Egyptology, has seen its principles gradually embraced by contemporary scholars - and well-read in esoterica and hermetic texts, Anyextee's insights into Luxor Temple are invaluable, offering a fresh perspective and enriching our understanding of this ancient marvel.

In this context, I resonate with the sentiment masterfully expressed by Anyextee in his work: "The Adept Initiate's Guide to Luxor Temple: Experiencing The Temple of Man Using The Esoteric Symbolist Approach." This guide transcends the ordinary, offering a synthesis of scholarly insight and spiritual profundity. It is not just a typical tourist guidebook or a dry academic volume; instead, it presents a unique blend appealing to both enthusiastic tourists and discerning scholars. It is, without doubt, the most comprehensive, contemporary and insightful guide to Luxor Temple, combining scholarly insight with spiritual depth in an unparalleled manner. By providing a deeper understanding of its esoteric essence, it serves as a significant contribution to the field of Egyptology. It offers both novices and scholars alike a fresh perspective on one of Egypt's most iconic monuments.

It is with great pleasure and honor that I introduce this seminal work. May this guide serve as a key to unlocking the hidden dimensions of Luxor Temple, offering readers not just knowledge, but an experience that resonates with the soul. Embark on this journey with an open heart and mind, and discover the ancient wisdom that has inspired civilizations for millennia.

ACKNOWLEDGEMENTS

In the process of creating this book, a journey that transcended mere distance to delve into profound realms of exploration and understanding, my heart is filled with gratitude. This gratitude spans not only those who have accompanied me on this path but also the invisible forces that have guided each step of the way.

I extend my deepest reverence and thanks to the One, the Absolute, the undifferentiated consciousness, and the primordial scission that paved the way for all of existence. Your unseen guidance has been the cornerstone of my journey.

To my parents, the initial guardians of my consciousness, I am forever grateful. Your love has illuminated my path from the start. I am equally thankful to Karina and Trinity, who introduced me to miracles I never thought possible.

The Symbolist School, deeply rooted in the teachings of Rene Schwaller de Lubicz, Lucie Lamy, and Alexandre Varille, laid the foundation of this work. A special tribute goes to my dear friend and mentor, symbolist author John Anthony West, who not only revealed to me the esoteric depths of symbolism but also supported my early endeavors. Our shared experiences in Egypt are etched in my memory as truly unforgettable.

I am grateful to my adored Egyptian sister, Sohaila Hussein for gracefully yielding the stage in our Symbolist Egypt dance, allowing my own light to shine. I'm deeply appreciative to my cherished Egyptian brothers - Ihab Rashid, for bringing the magic of "Heka" to life in Egypt, and Yousef Rashid, for his assistance. My appreciation extends to Emad Sayed, Al Dabaa Mo Hamada, and Gamal Nasir Afifi - fundamental pillars of support, whose friendship has been of immeasurable value.

I owe a debt of gratitude to Ken Lawrence at SailingstoneTravel.com, whose advice, challenges, and guidance were instrumental in the creation of this book. Adrian Baxter deserves a special mention for his unique illustration and design that grace the cover of this book, perfectly capturing its esoteric essence.

I am thankful for Sayed Mostafa, who provided me with a rare opportunity to guide the inspector of Luxor Temple through the Temple of Man using the unconventional esoteric symbolist approach. I'm eternally thankful for Laird (and Risa) Scranton, Matt Sibson, Ian Driscoll, Christopher Dunn, Glenn Kreisberg, Todd Hayen, and Keith Hamilton for their critical insights into ancient wisdom. And I'm wholeheartedly thankful to Normandi Ellis for continuing the legacy of support that was extended to my mentor's seminal work.

The Rosicrucian research library provided invaluable resources and the teachings of The Rosicrucian Order, A.M.O.R.C. contributed to polishing this philosopher's stone. Grand Master Julie Scott has been one of the most influential teachers on this student's path, albeit unknowingly, and I am immensely grateful for her influence. Chris Barton supplied the crucial image of a transparent block when I was blocked from my books, thereby significantly enriching this one.

I also wish to acknowledge the keepers, inspectors, and security personnel of Luxor Temple for their dedication to preserving this ancient wonder; the generous donors to my GoFundMe campaign, who helped turn this dream into a reality; Richard St. Pierre, for recognizing my potential to carry the torch for the Symbolist School's legacy; and Denise Gale, for offering sanctuary when it was most needed.

Gratitude is due to the AdeptInitiates.com community and AncientEgyptMysterySchools.com members, who pressed to delineate this knowledge not only for their understanding but because they recognized its relevance to others. And an equal amount of gratitude must go to the participants of Adept-Expeditions.com, whose support and enthusiasm are the fuel for our collective exploration.

This book is a mosaic, each piece a contribution from individuals who added their unique color and texture to the whole. To everyone mentioned and those unnamed who have touched this journey, my heart is brimming with gratitude. Together, we forge ahead, unraveling the mysteries of the past in pursuit of understanding, enlightenment, and connection. Thank you for joining me on this extraordinary voyage.

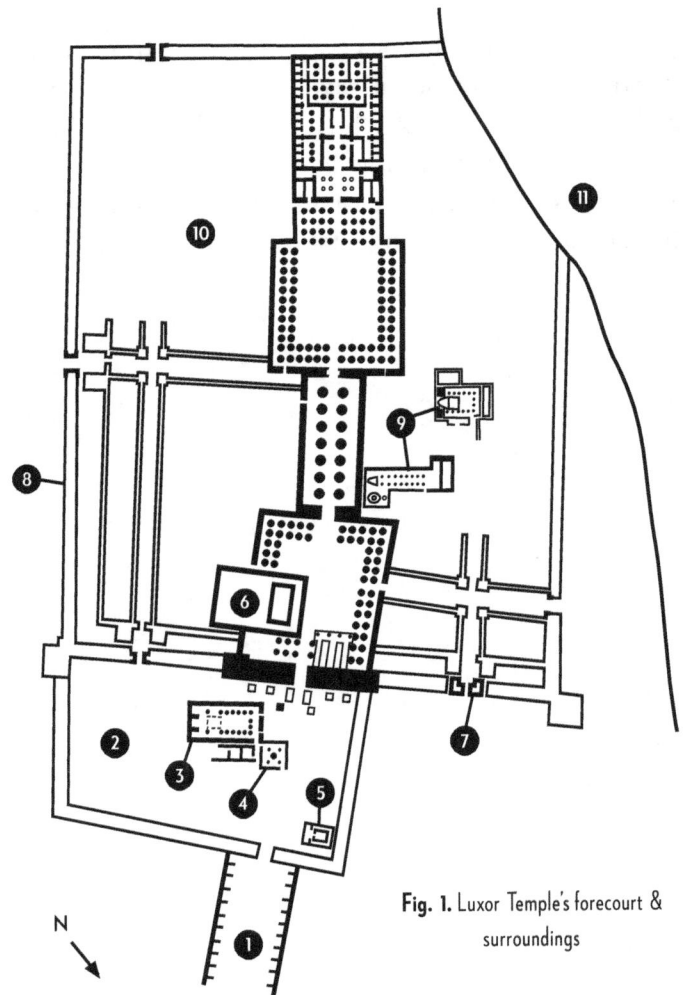

Fig. 1. Luxor Temple's forecourt & surroundings

N

1: *The Avenue of the Sphinxes*
2: *The Forecourt of Nectanebo*
3: *Coptic Church*
4: *Kiosk of Shabaqa*
5: *Serapis Chapel*
6: *Abu el-Haggag Mosque*

7. *Roman Camp Remains*
8: *Fortification Wall*
9: *Coptic Churches*
10: *The Open-Air Museum*
11: *The Nile River*

Fig. 2. The temple plan

1: *The Obelisk*
2: *The Ramesses II Colossi*
3: *The Shrine of Hatshepsut*
4: *The Court of Ramesses II*
5: *The Colonnade*
6: *The Peristyle Court*
7: *The Hypostyle Hall*
8: *The Chapel of Khonsu*
9: *The Chapel of Mut*
10: *The Chapel of Amun*
11: *The Chamber of the Divine Kings*
12: *The Offering Vestibule*
13: *The Hall of Theogamy*
14: *The Central Barque Shrine*
15: *The Hall of Twelve Columns*
16: *The Triple Sanctuary*

N

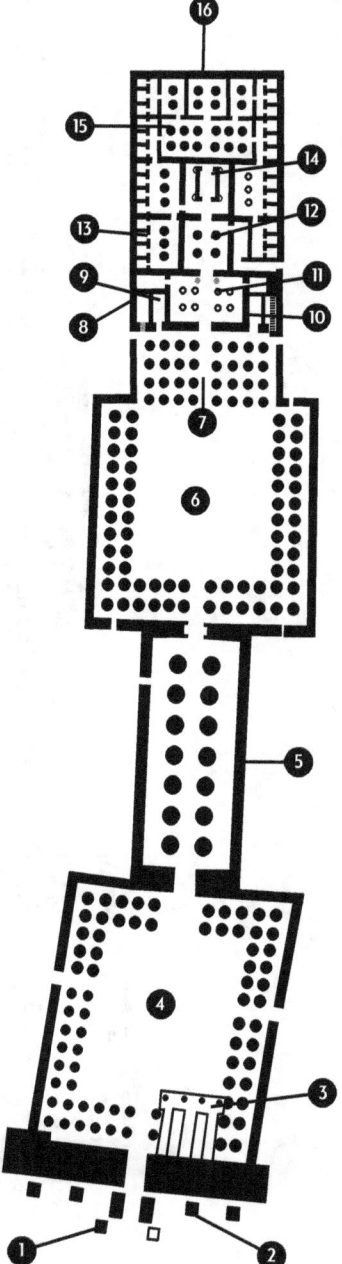

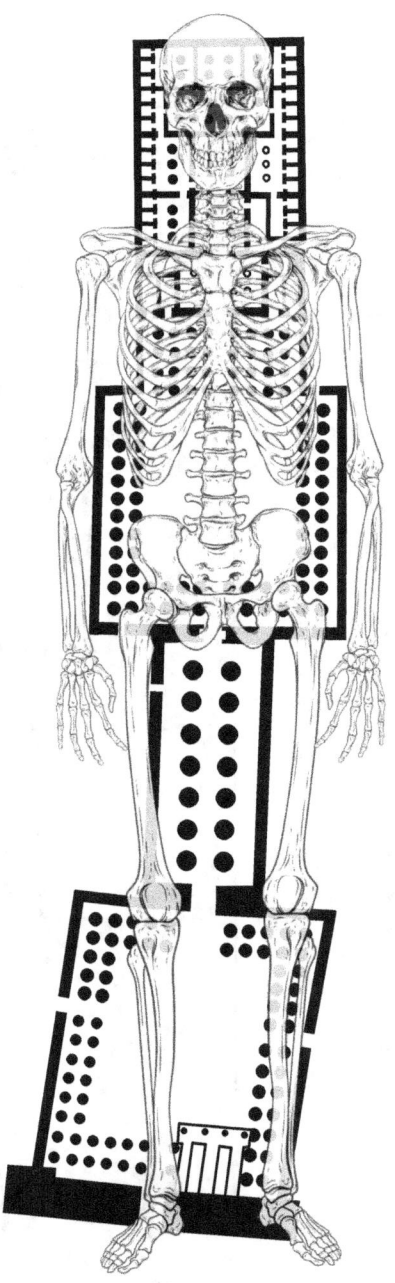

Fig. 3. A human skeleton superimposed over the Luxor Temple map

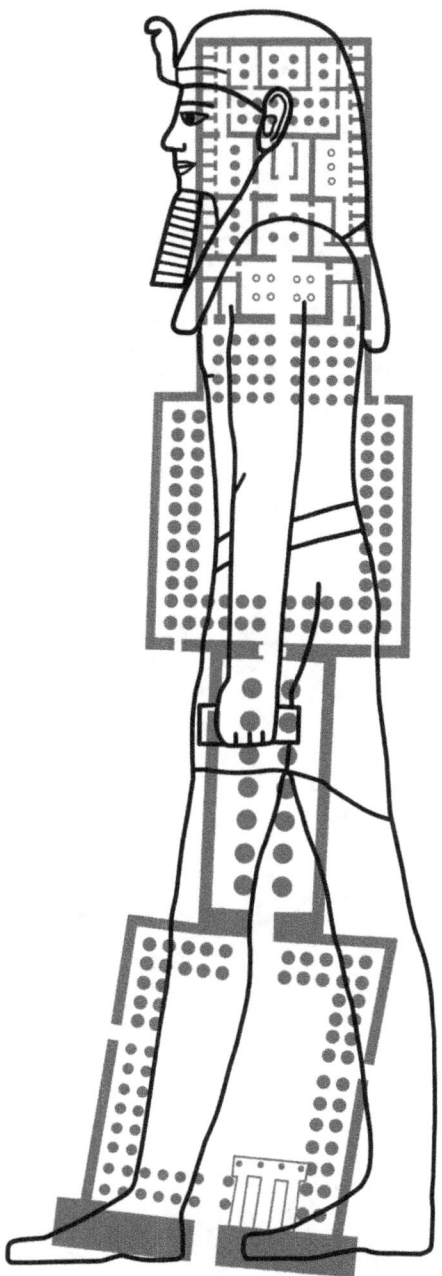

Fig. 4. A striding pharaoh superimposed over the temple map

INTRODUCTION

We often consider subjects like archaeology and anthropology to be nothing more than studies of the past, especially when it comes to civilizations like the ancient Egyptians, who existed thousands of years ago in a world very different from our own.

While we can still go today and marvel at their magnificent structures, many think of these ruins simply as lost remnants of a long-gone society, with little relevance to the here and now.

But thanks to the groundbreaking work of French chemist, alchemist and esotericist R.A. Schwaller de Lubicz (1887-1961), it's become abundantly clear that we still have much to learn from the ancient Egyptians that can aid us in the present.

While Schwaller wrote about nearly every facet of ancient Egypt, his main focus was Luxor Temple. To the Egyptians, he argued, the temple was not merely a place of worship, but a living school dedicated to man and his role in the cosmos.

When constructing their temples, the Egyptians did not merely attempt to create something aesthetically pleasing. Rather, everything from a temple's dimensions to the number of columns to the placement of particular blocks of stone were all deliberately carried out with a greater teaching in mind.

Schwaller referred to this Pharaonic philosophy as the Sacred Science. And while the pharaohs may be long gone, the Sacred Science is as relevant as ever, as it deals with the fundamental laws of the universe and man's relationship to them. Though some of its reliefs may have faded and its rooftops partially collapsed,

Luxor Temple remains an invaluable tool for studying the Sacred Science even thousands of years after it was built.

As important as R.A. Schwaller de Lubicz's books are, they're by no means easy reads. In the 1970s, writer, researcher and tour guide John Anthony West helped make Schwaller's teachings more palatable to a wider audience with his book *Serpent in The Sky*. To this day, it remains the best overall introduction to Schwaller's work and, moreover, the philosophy of the ancient Egyptians.

Now in the 21st century, my aim with this book is to keep the torch of the esoteric tradition lit, guiding a new generation of travelers and seekers looking to experience Luxor Temple through the eyes of the symbolist.

Largely based on the work of Schwaller and West, my personal mentor, this book will guide you through each part of the temple, explaining it all from both a historic and symbolist perspective. But it also brings a plethora of new information to the table.

Not only will you get the latest information based on recent archaeological findings, but you'll find a detailed summary of the reliefs of each room, together with translations of some of the most important hieroglyphic inscriptions.

Taking things a step further, included at the end is a Practical Applications section which draws from numerous esoteric and mystical traditions. These exercises help one directly experience the Temple of Man, going beyond just understanding it on a cerebral level. As you make your way deeper into the temple, you'll be guided through a variety of meditation, visualization and mindfulness techniques

Fig. 5. Amun, the "Invisible One"

that you can try at your own pace.

Anyone today may be able to buy a ticket and walk through Luxor Temple, but touring the Temple of Man through the symbolist perspective could be thought of as a sacred initiation. Not only will the experience help you broaden your understanding of the mindset of the ancients, but entering the temple is a step forward toward learning more about yourself.

WHO WAS R. A. SCHWALLER DE LUBICZ?

········ ☥ ········

Born on 30 December 1887 in Strasbourg, René Adolphe Schwaller de Lubicz would go on to forever change the way we think about ancient Egypt. It's thanks to Schwaller that we can finally confirm what was long suspected by countless philosophers, esotericists and artists over the last few thousand years.

Schwaller's work proves that the Egyptians possessed a deep understanding of life's greatest mysteries, such as creation, universal laws and man's true relationship with the cosmos. But rather than express these ideas explicitly in writing, they encoded this secret knowledge in their myths, artwork and the proportions of their buildings.

When examining his upbringing and various talents, we can see that few could've been more qualified to "crack the code" of ancient Egypt than Schwaller de Lubicz.

Schwaller was the son of a pharmacist of Swiss-German origin, and he grew up fluent in both French and German. He spent much of his youth conducting chemical experiments in his father's laboratory, but he was also in touch with his creative side, dedicating much of his free time to painting.

Ever since he was a boy, he contemplated the mysteries of the universe, such as the origin of matter and the role which numbers play in creation. These preoccupations would greatly influence the course of his life, ultimately drawing him to Egypt.

Fig. 6. Strasbourg, France, the birthplace of Schwaller de Lubicz

In 1904, Schwaller left the Alsace region, which at the time was controlled by Germany, in order to evade mandatory military service. In the dark of night, he crossed the border and escaped to Paris, where he would stay with his aunt.

Earning a living as a chemist for a coal company, it was in Paris that he'd encounter many important figures who would help shape his thinking over the years. In 1908, he began attending the school of Henri Matisse, an influential artist known for his color theories. And from 1913-16, Schwaller would become involved with the local branch of the Theosophical Society, the esoteric movement founded by Russian spiritualist Helena Blavatsky in the 19th century.

At the time, most of those in France with an interest in esotericism or the occult were involved with Theosophy in some shape or form. And it's through Theosophy that Schwaller would come into contact with various alchemists. But what exactly is alchemy?

For some, it can mean devising ways to transform matter, such as turning base metals into gold. For others, alchemy refers to an internal process which involves the cultivation and transmutation of vital energies. For Schwaller de Lubicz, a chemist with a deep interest in spirituality, it was both.

During World War I, despite being born a German citizen, Schwaller would work as a lab technician for the French army. And following the war, he'd depart from the Theosophical Society to form his own initiatory group known as *Les Veilleurs*, or "The Watchers."

Naturally, the Great War prompted deep reflection in those who lived through it. Schwaller came to believe that the gradual mechanization of European society was causing it to lose its soul. And one of his main objectives at the time was preserving the traditional role of the artisan.

Accordingly, it was around this time that Schwaller would become deeply immersed in the study of Gothic cathedrals. Collaborating with artist and inventor Jean-Julien Champagne (1877–1932), a fellow member of The Watchers, the two sought to recreate the techniques used to make the stained glass of cathedrals like Chartres. Convinced that the medieval artisans were using long-lost alchemical processes, Scwhaller and Champagne were determined to rediscover them.

And through their study of Gothic cathedrals, the pair came to see these masterworks not merely as aesthetically pleasing buildings, but as initiatory texts in three-dimensional form. As we'll cover over the course of this book, Schwaller would later go on to study the temples of Egypt from the same perspective.

Some researchers have speculated that the legendary French alchemist Fulcanelli – whose true identity remains unconfirmed to this day – was really Schwaller's colleague Jean-Julien Champagne. Interestingly, Schwaller once lent Champagne some of his unpublished notes, though his colleague warned him not to publish them, as they revealed too many secrets. Schwaller agreed. But years later, he was shocked to find that his work was used as the basis for *Le Mystère des Cathédrales*, published under Fulcanelli's name in 1926.

Another prominent figure of The Watchers was a Lithuanian nobleman and poet named Oskar Vladislas de Lubicz Milosz. According to multiple sources, following the war, Schwaller helped

Fig. 7. The stained glass windows of Chartres

him devise a plan that would restore Lithuania's former borders, thus protecting the small country from the Bolsheviks. Feeling so indebted to Schwaller's contributions, Milosz formally adopted him into his clan, which was known as both Boza-wola ("Will of God") and de Lubicz. John Anthony West, on the other hand, claimed that Schwaller's stepdaughter Lucie Lamy told him the honor was bestowed on Schwaller for curing Milosz's lupus. In any case, from that point on, René Adolphe Schwaller would be officially known as R. A. Schwaller de Lubicz.

A few years later in 1922, Schwaller de Lubicz and his entourage moved to the area of St. Moritz, Switzerland, the same place that Nietzsche had made his summer home in the 1880s. It was here that they established the *Station Scientifique de Suhalia*, or Suhalia Laboratories. It was meant to be a center of study where initiates could practice various arts, sciences and occult practices away from the hustle and bustle of the modern world.

It was around this time that Schwaller would take on the pseudonym Aor, which means "light" in Hebrew and "gold" in French. And it was also during this period that Schwaller would marry his second wife, Isha (1885-1963), who'd remain by his side up until his passing.

Eventually, the money to maintain Suhalia would run dry, and so Schwaller and Isha relocated to southern France, where he further developed his alchemical color theory.

Isha, an author with a long-held interest in a diverse range of theological and mystical teachings, was especially passionate about ancient Egypt. And upon her prompting, the couple decided to move to Egypt in 1936.

Like many European occultists, Schwaller and Isha suspected that the true root of Pythagorean ideas and the western esoteric tradition lie in ancient Egypt. Armed with an extensive knowledge of chemistry, alchemy, art and architecture, they would go on to meticulously study the Egyptian temples of Luxor to determine how much the ancient Egyptians really knew.

Schwaller was particularly interested in whether or not the Egyptians were aware of phi, or the Golden Section, well before the Greeks were. And by measuring the temples and their artwork, Schwaller could confirm that the ancient Egyptians did indeed utilize phi in their temple proportions and in their two-dimensional art. Though, unlike the Greeks, they never wrote this knowledge down.

While his symbolist theories clashed with those of traditional Egyptology, Schwaller nevertheless attracted a group of like-minded individuals during his time in Egypt. Together they'd become known as *Le Groupe de Louxor*, members of which included Schwaller's stepdaughter Lucie Lamy, Valley of the Kings guardian Alexandre Stoppeläre, and Egyptologist Alexandre Varille.

Varille served as the main link between the symbolist school and academic Egyptology. But following his sudden tragic death in 1951, this dialog came to an end.

Nevertheless, Schwaller's work in Egypt would gain notoriety in France beyond academic circles. In 1949, avant-garde filmmaker Jean Cocteau took an interest in Schwaller's symbolist theories and helped popularize them in Europe. And years later, Schwaller would be invited to present at the Congrès de Symbolistes organized by André Breton, co-founder of the Surrealist movement.

All in all, Schwaller would spend twelve years living in Egypt and would continue to write about Egypt and its symbolism for the remainder of his life. As we'll cover throughout this guide, his main area of focus was Luxor Temple, on which he wrote two groundbreaking books.

He first presented a summary of his research in the relatively brief *The Temple in Man: Sacred Architecture and the Perfect Man*, which he later followed up with the multivolume *Le Temple de l'Homme*, or *The Temple of Man* - easily his most important work.

But despite being the first modern scholar to convincingly decode the pharaonic mindset and the lost teachings of ancient Egypt, Schwaller de Lubicz's research would largely go unnoticed outside of France. That is until American writer and researcher John Anthony West presented Schwaller's ideas to the English-speaking world for the first time in the 1970s.

WHO WAS JOHN ANTHONY WEST?

Born in 1932 in New York, John Anthony West was living on the Spanish island of Ibiza when he first encountered the work of George Gurdjieff. Entranced by the Russian mystic and philosopher's writings, he left Ibiza for London to join the Gurdjieff Foundation. And it was there that he'd encounter the works of another author that would change his life forever: R. A. Schwaller de Lubicz.

Painstakingly reading through and translating Schwaller's multiple books to grasp their essence, John Anthony West would end up creating a masterpiece in its own right: *Serpent in the Sky: The High Wisdom of Ancient Egypt*. The influential book was

Fig. 8. Di Ankh ("To give life") - Long live the work of J.A.W.

released in 1978 before any of Schwaller's books had been published in English. Condensed into a single volume, West managed to summarize Schwaller's main theories and discoveries while making them palpable to the modern reader.

While most of Schwaller's books are now available in English, they're by no means easy reads. *Serpent in the Sky*, therefore, continues to serve as the best introduction to his work.

West would also gain notoriety for his research on the Great Sphinx of Giza, championing the controversial theory that the sculpture is thousands of years older than commonly believed. While Schwaller himself didn't write much on the subject, he did briefly note his observation that the Sphinx was probably eroded by water and not sand.

This offhand comment prompted West to visit Egypt with respected geologist Dr. Robert M. Schoch. Schoch would confirm Schwaller's observation, and the duo's new controversial hypothesis sent shockwaves throughout the world of Egyptology.

In the 1980s, John Anthony West would also publish a travel guide called *The Traveler's Key to Ancient Egypt*, in which he presented the symbolist perspective in travel book form.

But while considerably more accessible than Schwaller's original writings, the concepts presented by West in his books can still be difficult to grasp at times. That's where this book, which was largely inspired by *The Traveler's Key*'s chapter on Luxor Temple, comes in.

For the rest of his life, West would also lead symbolist study tours to Egypt in person, some of which I had the privilege of attending and filming. This participation led me to create my original video series called Ancient Egypt Mystery Schools. We got to know each other over the years, and I came to consider him a dear friend and mentor.

We kept in regular contact, and he generously made himself available to answer my endless questions. He would assign me research projects and provide me with the appropriate book recommendations. Working with West was a conscious-expanding experience that conferred a deeply profound impact on my being. And the current of that impact continues to echo through my work today.

In 2018, John Anthony West would transition to the afterlife at the age of 85. But he, like Schwaller de Lubicz, still continues to aid and inspire people around the world on their quests for Truth. And it's largely thanks to these two men that *The Adept Initiate's Guide to Luxor Temple* could come to fruition.

THE SYMBOLIST APPROACH

> Through symbolism, and through it alone can we read the thought of the Ancients. It is only through the symbolical that we will be able to coordinate the known elements of this great civilization and that the writing may take on its true meaning. - R.A. Schwaller de Lubicz[1]

Egypt's largest temple, and one of the largest religious structures in the world, is Karnak, which lies on the east bank of the Nile in Luxor. The massive temple complex could be considered an homage to creation itself - the physical manifestation of matter during what Schwaller de Lubicz calls the Primordial Scission.

According to Schwaller, the Egyptians believed in a scission that occurred when a single, unified and infinite reality began the process of dividing itself, resulting in what we now experience as polarity, matter, time and space. And when examined carefully through Schwaller's symbolist approach, we can see that every portion of Karnak Temple was intended to represent a different aspect of creation.

Luxor Temple, on the other hand, which lies just two kilometers down the river from Karnak, was built as an homage to man. After taking precise measurements of every element of the temple and then comparing it with the proportions of an anatomically correct skeleton, Schwaller made an amazing discovery: Each section of Luxor Temple corresponds precisely to a part of the human body.

But Luxor Temple is much more than a map of the human form. Rather, it's meant to teach us how the cosmic forces of creation are present within all of us, and in turn, our role in the greater macrocosm.

Fig. 9.
Sekhmet, a symbol of both healing and destruction

The symbols utilized to express this, however, are far from obvious. And that's where this guide comes in. Over the course of this book, we'll be examining each portion of the temple and what it signifies on an anatomical, cosmological and spiritual level.

With that being said, as Schwaller constantly stresses in his books, no single part of Luxor Temple can be understood in isolation. The true teaching of the temple can only be realized when examining it as a whole.

In ancient Egyptian times, access to Luxor Temple would've been strictly limited to a select few initiates of the priesthood along with members of the royal family. But even though the temple is now accessible to all, thousands of visitors come and go each year, none the wiser to its real meaning.

Exploring Luxor Temple from the symbolist approach, then, is the closest we can come to stepping into the sandals of an ancient Egyptian priest.

> The Temple tells, in stone, in its proportions and harmonies, its art and sculpture, the story of the creation of man; it signals his development, stage by stage, and it recreates in artistic form man's relationship to the universe. - John Anthony West[2]

A BRIEF HISTORY OF LUXOR TEMPLE

. . . . ☥ . . . .

The location on which Luxor Temple now stands was once home to a small temple established during Egypt's Middle Kingdom period (1975-1640 BC). It was also the Middle Kingdom pharaohs who initiated the first constructions at nearby Karnak. But Luxor Temple as we know it largely took form during Egypt's 18th Dynasty (1550-1290 BC), the first dynasty of the prosperous New Kingdom period (1550-c. 1077 BC).

The 18th Dynasty was arguably the most significant Egyptian dynasty since the 4th Dynasty, those responsible for the pyramids at Giza. And it's easily Egyptian history's most drama-filled.

The dynasty was founded by Pharaoh Ahmose I, who finally expelled the foreign Hyksos rulers that had controlled Egypt for around a century. It's no surprise then, that with bitter memories of being ruled by foreigners still fresh in their minds, the 18th Dynasty pharaohs adopted an aggressive expansionist policy.

Pharaohs like Thutmosis I and Thutmosis III would greatly expand Egypt's territory, transforming it from a kingdom to an empire for the first time. And speaking of Thutmosis III (r. 1479-

1425 BC), his reign began as a co-regent with his aunt Hatshepsut, Egypt's longest-reigning female pharaoh. To this day, the true nature of their relationship remains a hotly debated topic amongst Egyptologists and history buffs alike.

As we'll cover shortly, the oldest extant structure at Luxor Temple is a small shrine that was likely erected during Hatshepsut and Thutmosis III's joint reign, which we'll be referring to as the Shrine of Hatshepsut. While at first glance minor and insignificant, this shrine may play a much more important role in Luxor Temple's design scheme than first meets the eye (see p112).

The 18th Dynasty also brought us the bizarre Amarna period, during which Amenhotep IV, better known as Akhenaten, would drastically change the Egyptian religion and create a brand new art style. Additionally, he'd even alter the written language to mirror the contemporary style of speaking.

After moving the capital from Luxor to the virgin desert of Amarna, his "revolution" would fail to take hold long-term – at least in Egypt itself. According to Rosicrucian literature, Akhenaten's philosophy of Atenism would go on to influence major world religions and spiritual movements for centuries to come.

Be that as it may, the Egyptian religion and art style would already begin returning to the status quo during the reign of his successor, Tutankhamun.

But just prior to the radical changes brought forth by the Amarna period, Egypt enjoyed three decades of stability and prosperity. The reign of Amenhotep III (c. 1388-1350 BC), in

Fig. 10. A statue of Amenhotep III discovered at Luxor Temple

fact, is regarded by many scholars as the zenith of art, culture and political power of New Kingdom Egypt.

Throughout his illustrious reign, Amenhotep III initiated large-scale building campaigns which included his massive mortuary temple. Though mostly lost to time and natural disasters, it's believed to have been Egypt's largest-ever temple upon its completion. Today, little more than the Colossi of Memnon statues remain.

In addition to constructing a large royal palace for himself, he also made further contributions to the ever-growing Karnak Temple. But surely his greatest work was Luxor Temple - the focus of this book and what's arguably a masterpiece on par with the pyramids of Giza.

The temple's designer was a most enlightened man named Amenhotep, son of Hapu (there were many Amenhoteps in those days), the pharaoh's head priest, scribe and architect. Starting his career as a military scribe, he gradually rose through the ranks, becoming the pharaoh's right-hand man for both civilian and military projects.

As the ancient Egyptians kept the design plans and building methods of their pyramids and temples top secret, we'll never know just how Amenhotep, son of Hapu devised his master plan. But as you experience

Fig. 11. A statue of Amenhotep, son of Hapu from Karnak

the temple - both through this book and in-person - the architect's genius will soon become apparent.

Interestingly, he, along with 3rd Dynasty architect Imhotep, are among the few non-royals in Egypt to have ever been deified. Following his death, commoners that were barred entry into Karnak Temple would instead pray to a statue of Amenhotep, son of Hapu that had been placed outside.

Amenhotep, son of Hapu wouldn't end up living to see the completion of his creation. Following the interruption of the Amarna period, Tutankhamun would resume work on the Colonnade. Further decorations were then added by his successors, ranging from Ay to Seti I, who would complete the Colonnade's wall carvings and columns within a few decades of Tut's death.

Seti's son, Ramesses II (1279-1213 BC), who's widely regarded as Egypt's most prolific ever builder, would go on to finally complete the temple. He contributed a large court and pylon - albeit on a skewed axis from the rest of the temple. While the design choice has long puzzled scholars, Schwaller de Lubicz believed that Ramesses was merely carrying out a plan that had been in place since the temple's inception.

Even after the fall of the New Kingdom, Luxor Temple would remain in use for centuries. The outer court saw additions in the 25th Dynasty, while Nectanebo II (381-340 BC), Egypt's last native-born pharaoh, further added to the forecourt.

What's more, is that visitors to Luxor Temple can observe additions by Alexander the Great and the Romans. And it was subsequently utilized by the Coptic Christians and Muslims. In fact, as you'll observe during your visit, the mosque constructed within the Court of Ramesses II remains in use to this day.

THE INITIATE'S GUIDE

*T*his section of the book takes you step by step through the temple, covering the history and symbolism of each area, along with the significance of many of the hieroglyphs and reliefs.

Before your visit to Luxor, it's recommended to read through this guide at least once. Then, as you explore the temple, having this book in hand will open up a new dimension to the ancient structure that few visitors experience.

But even if you can't make it to Egypt in the near future, this Initiate's Guide can serve as the next best thing to touring Luxor Temple in person. You'll gain vital knowledge about the temple and its message, and perhaps even be able to integrate some of its teachings into your everyday life.

THE AVENUE OF THE SPHINXES

For many years, visitors traveling between Karnak and Luxor Temple would either have to do so by private vehicle or a walk through the hectic streets of modern Luxor. But now, after years of restoration work, the ancient 2.7 km-long processional way linking the temples is finally open to the public.

Currently known as Al-Kebbash Road, the ancient Egyptians called this road *wat neteru*, or "The Path of Gods." And it was along this path that the sacred barque and golden statue of Amun would be carried to Luxor Temple as part of an annual religious procession known as the Opet Festival. Interestingly, the festival, which celebrated the annual flooding of the Nile, predates Luxor Temple's foundation.

It was likely Hatshepsut (r. 1473-1458 BC) who first began work on the Avenue of the Sphinxes. In fact, it was her Red Chapel, as it's now known by archaeologists, that provides us with the earliest images of the Opet Festival. Originally placed in front of Karnak's Holy of Holies, the Red Chapel was dismantled by later pharaohs and reassembled by archaeologists in modern times. It now stands in Karnak's Open-Air Museum.

The chapel's reliefs reveal that the sacred barque of Amun would stop at six way stations along the road, undergoing ritual cleansings at each. Upon reaching the area of what was to become Luxor Temple, the barque would then be transported back to Karnak by boat.

Amenhotep III (r. 1388-1350 BC), the pharaoh who would commission Luxor Temple, would then continue working on the avenue. He would extend the sacred road to link Luxor Temple with the Temple of Khonsu, situated in the southern portion of the massive Karnak temple complex.

The sculptures discovered near the Temple of Khonsu, in fact are the oldest of all those found along the Avenue of the Sphinxes.

Fig. 12. A modern replica of an ancient barque shrine

Fig. 13. Looking down the Avenue of the Sphinxes

But they're not sphinxes. Instead, the sculptures depict full-bodied rams, for reasons we'll discuss shortly. Amenhotep III, in fact, placed no less than 120 crouching ram statues near Karnak.

The next pharaoh to contribute to the Avenue of the Sphinxes would be Tutankhamun (r. 1332-1323 BC). As mentioned earlier, Tutankhamun would undo many of the changes of the Amarna period, restoring the traditional religion of ancient Egypt. And in addition to his contributions to Luxor Temple, he would also add 130 new ram-headed sculptures to the avenue.

But in contrast to the full-bodied rams of his grandfather, these were criosphinxes, or sculptures with a ram's head on a lion's body. These would stretch from Karnak's tenth pylon, situated just east of the Temple of Khonsu, to the Precinct of Mut, located further south. Later pharaohs such as Ay and Horemheb would usurp some of these sculptures, adding their own cartouches.

The next addition to the avenue wouldn't come until the reign of Ramesses II (1279-1213 BC), the final major contributor to Luxor Temple. By this time, the annual Opet Festival had gotten longer, extending to a full month of festivities. And during the 19th Dynasty, the procession would begin from Karnak Temple's second pylon, located near the present-day entrance at the temple's west. At this processional avenue, Ramesses II would place additional criosphinxes.

But the Avenue of the Sphinxes was no longer used for the Opet Festival by this time, and hadn't since at least the reign of Tutankhamun. By the 19th Dynasty, the roundtrip procession would take place entirely by boat. The avenue would, however, continue to host the annual Procession of Mut.

A few centuries later, the next pharaoh to add to the avenue would be Pinedjem I (r. 1070-1032 BC) of the 21st Dynasty, part of the tumultuous era that historians now call the Third Intermediate Period. Pinedjem would move some of the full-bodied ram statues placed by Amenhotep III a short distance to the front of the Temple of Khonsu's pylon (fig. 14). It was also Penidjem that would move many of the criosphinxes of both Amenhotep III and Ramesses II to create a new east-west avenue from Karnak's second pylon to the temple's quay (fig. 15). These criosphinxes, in fact, are first thing visitors see when approaching Karnak Temple today.

The next major additions to the avenue came several centuries later during the reign of Nectanebo I (r. 379-361 BC) of the 30th Dynasty. Over a millennium after its initial establishment, he'd go on to renovate and expand the Avenue of the Sphinxes, bringing it to a total length of 2,220 meters. And Nectanebo I would also add no less than 807 androsphinxes, or sculptures of a man's head on a lion's body - what we typically picture when we think of a sphinx.

The faces on these sphinxes likely depict Nectanebo himself, though some scholars take them to represent Amenhotep III, the temple's original builder (fig. 16). (Given the presence of androsphinxes of Hatshepsut's likeness at her mortuary temple in Deir el Bahari, it's possible that she once placed similar sculptures along the Avenue of the Sphinxes, though no such evidence yet exists.)

The 30th Dynasty would be the last group of native-born Egyptian pharaohs to rule over the country. Nevertheless, the Avenue of the Sphinxes would continue to be traversed for centuries thereafter. Thanks to the discovery of a cartouche during recent excavations, we now know that Cleopatra herself walked down this road during her journeys with Marc Antony in the 1st century BC.

Today, the recently restored avenue stretches out to 2,700 meters long and 70 meters wide. And it's currently home to no less than 1,060 sculptures, of which there are three different types. But what do they signify? Let's take a deeper look into the Avenue of the Sphinxes' symbolism and how it relates to the overall teachings of both Karnak and Luxor Temple.

THE SYMBOLISM OF THE SPHINXES

As mentioned, the first statues to be added near Karnak were those of full-bodied rams, followed by criosphinxes and then androsphinxes. All three types can still be seen by visitors today. But due to various remodelings by later pharaohs, you won't see one form smoothly transition to the next along a straight path.

Fig. 14. A full-bodied ram near Karnak

Fig. 15. Criosphinxes at the entrance to Karnak

Nevertheless, one can still contemplate the secret meaning behind all three forms and their relationship to one another.

First off is the ram, a symbol of Amun, the prominent deity worshipped during Egypt's New Kingdom period, and a personification of the creative force responsible for all life (fig. 5). Much like Ra during the Old Kingdom period, Amun came to represent the concept of the Absolute, or the perfect state of Unity that existed before creation.

The full-bodied ram statues near Karnak, therefore, should best be thought of as representatives of the Absolute - a concept which cannot be observed or comprehended in a normal state of consciousness. These sculptures can currently be found near Karnak's Temple of Khonsu, right near where Amenhotep III placed them.

Next are the criosphinxes, or sculptures consisting of a ram's head on a lion's body. The lion itself was long regarded as a solar symbol. And the lion's body, with the animal's signature characteristics of might and power, represents the concept of spiritual energy made manifest as physical – much like how the Egyptians viewed the sun itself.

The ram-headed sphinx could thus be interpreted as the Absolute descending from a perfect state of Oneness into our physical world of time and space. The ram head's downward pointed horns here may denote this descent from pure spirit into matter. As mentioned, criosphinxes can be seen outside of Karnak's main entrance, as well as the complex's southern portion leading to the Precinct of Mut.

Finally, all along the main avenue toward Luxor Temple, the Temple of Man, we encounter hundreds of androsphinxes, or sculptures of a pharaoh's head atop a lion's body. The royal human head here represents human consciousness and its participation in the divine, of which it is an emanation.

In other words, this artistic synthesis could be viewed as a metaphor for how the divine source experiences itself via the human experience. The Great Sphinx of Giza, for example, was nicknamed Ra-Horakhty – a fusion of Ra, the primordial source of creation, and Horus, who represents the state of the Perfected Man.

The human-faced sphinx, therefore, should be thought of as a symbol of a Perfected Man rather than the ordinary state of human consciousness. This symbol serves as an important reminder of how we all possess a latent ability within us to achieve this higher state of consciousness – the goal of nearly every major religion.

In various world traditions, this state of perfection has been referred to as terms like Samadhi, gnosis, cosmic bliss, self realization, and in Rosicrucian terminology, the Rose-Croix state or Peace Profound. While we don't know exactly what the Egyptians called it, progress toward achieving this state was clearly an integral part of their art, architecture and overall approach to life.

Additionally, sphinxes, which depict a fusion of man and wild animal, may also represent man's taming of his animal instincts, or "lower self." This concept of self-mastery is emphasized in numerous world traditions by means of various symbols.

One notable example is the Masonic symbol of the ashlar, a rough stone taken directly from the quarry which represents the uninitiated. The "perfect ashlar," on the other hand, is a stone that has been smoothed and polished, representing the initiate who, through long periods of education, diligence and "inner alchemy," has mastered the secret teachings.

Similarly, Chinese culture has long regarded the act of polishing rough jade as a metaphor for self-development. And speaking of jade, the Mayan culture of Mesoamerica also used the green stone to represent the self-realized man. For example, in the funerary garb of King Pakal discovered at Palenque, the king was found holding a jade cube in one hand and a sphere in another. Symbolically, "squaring the circle" means seeing equally in four different directions: up, down, inwardly and outwardly.

Fig. 16. An androsphinx, likely depicting Nectanebo I

"Egypt evoked, but never explained," writes John Anthony West.[2] But it would seem that the core message of these stone sphinxes correlates closely with numerous metaphors, fables and symbols from sacred doctrines around the world. It is only by conquering our "animal self" through dedication and perseverance that we can ultimately partake with the divine.

In a more general sense, sphinxes were also regarded as protectors and guardians of sacred precincts. Not only did they offer physical protection, but also aid and guidance on a spiritual level.

As mentioned earlier, Karnak Temple was consecrated to creation itself at the time of the Primordial Scission. Luxor Temple, meanwhile, was consecrated to man's role in the greater macrocosm. Neither temple, therefore, should be looked at in isolation, as the teaching of one greatly compliments the other.

Today, as we walk down the Avenue of the Sphinxes from Karnak to Luxor, the symbols remind us of the Absolute dividing itself to experience existence in time and space, and then ultimately through human consciousness. And proceeding from Luxor Temple back towards Karnak, we're reminded of each soul's ultimate goal: a return to the divine source. Clearly, then, the Avenue of the Sphinxes is not merely decorative or practical, but an integral part of the deeper meanings behind the two temples which it connects.

But in contrast to the Great Sphinx of Giza, which, sits alone on the desert plateau, here we see the same imagery repeated over a thousand times. This repeated imagery could be likened to temple art across Asia, in which countless repetitions of the same image are meant to have a hypnotic effect on the observer - much like a visual mantra. Now accessible to the public for the first time since ancient times, the trance-inducing walk down the Avenue of the Sphinxes is something all visitors should experience at some point during their stay in Luxor.

THE OUTER PYLON & FORECOURT

········ ☥ ········

Approaching Luxor Temple from the Avenue of Sphinxes, the first architectural feature you'll observe is its large pylon which stretches out to 24 meters high by 64 meters wide. Pylons often demarcated a temple entrance, separating the inner, sacred world from the outer, profane realm of everyday life.

Not only was entry past this point restricted to a small group of initiates, but the priests would have to undergo a strict series of purification rituals before they could proceed any further.

Additionally, pylons served a variety of symbolic functions. First of all, they closely resemble the hieroglyph for Akhet, or horizon. The symbol appears as a sun rising between two mountain peaks in the distance.

The sunrise itself was deeply symbolic for the Egyptians, who saw it as a metaphor for spiritual resurrection. Furthermore, a

Fig. 17. Luxor Temple's pylon, colossi and obelisk

pylon's shape also represents unity splitting into duality at the time of the Primordial Scission.

While many Egyptologists believe that the two halves symbolize Isis and her sister Nephtys, Rosicrucians have long taught that the left pylon represents Isis and the right her husband Osiris, thus symbolizing the law of duality.

While missing today, ancient Egyptian pylons were designed with four vertical niches to hold wooden flagpoles. These would've been made of Lebanese cedar and fitted with sockets of Asiatic copper. The reason for the flagpoles becomes clear once we look at the hieroglyph for Neter (a deity or force of creation), which clearly resembles a flagpole! Not only were the Egyptians fond of symbolic wordplay, but they were adept at implementing it into their three-dimensional temple plans.

THE RELIEFS

In regards to human anatomy, Luxor Temple's outer pylon corresponds to the feet. And as you stand out front, take a look at the eastern (left) side of the pylon near the portal. Notice the nine pairs of horses, stacked vertically, pulling nine chariots driven by eight of Ramesses II's archers (fig. 18). At the spot where the ninth archer would appear, some stone has been chiseled out.

The bows in these archers' hands represent an ancient symbol known as the Nine Bows. Depicted in Egyptian art since as early as the Predynastic period (3200-3000 BC), the symbol served as a collective representation of Egypt's enemies - whomever they may have been at the time.

In art pieces like statue pedestals, the Nine Bows were often placed under the pharaoh's feet, symbolizing him trampling over the country's foes. Furthermore, the symbol was sometimes even depicted on the insoles of a pharaoh's sandals. It's appropriate then, that when a human body is superimposed over the temple plan, the Nine Bows appear directly under the feet!

Fig. 18. Archers representing the Nine Bows

Interestingly, while now lost, Schwaller also observed that the forecourt's outer walls would've been divided into nine distinct sections, each of which resembled a bow when seen from above.

As we'll go into more detail later, an interesting anatomical correspondence is represented by the width of the west pylon, which according to Schwaller measures out to 12 fathoms, or around 22 meters. Much deeper within the temple is a room featuring twelve columns that represents important cranial nerves. And that room is also 12 fathoms wide.

In the human body, the twelve pairs of cranial nerves are intricately linked to the big toe by the central nervous channel, and the symmetry in measurements here is surely a deliberate indication of this physiological connection.

One wonders if the ancient Egyptians also had an understanding of reflexology, or the practice of applying pressure to the feet in order to stimulate a corresponding organ elsewhere within the body. While Schwaller didn't comment on it, the pylon of Luxor Temple would certainly make for an interesting subject of future study.

Looking back at the reliefs, the nine chariots are far from the only warriors depicted here. A fascinating but little-known fact is that the bodyguards shown carrying long swords on the western pylon are not Egyptian, but Sardinian troops. Known as Shardana, the Egyptians frequently hired them as mercenaries.

But who is the Egyptian side fighting? As a whole, the battle scenes of the outer pylon represent an important historical event: the Battle of Kadesh.

At the time, Egypt, then led by Ramesses II, was vying for control over parts of the Middle East against the Anatolia-based Hittite Empire. Misinformed by a captured spy that his enemies were at Aleppo, Ramesses was ambushed upon his arrival in the city of Kadesh, modern-day Syria.

Entirely cut off from his troops, the pharaoh found himself alone on the battlefield. And according to legend, he channeled Amun, who suddenly inhabited his body, allowing him to lay waste to scores of enemy soldiers.

The Battle of Kadesh, which resulted in the world's first recorded peace treaty, was indeed a real event. But were the scenes on the outer pylon solely intended as political propaganda, or do they contain a deeper level of meaning?

According to the symbolist perspective, battle scenes were used as an allegory for temple initiates to contemplate the eternal struggle between light and darkness. "Having vanquished the enemy, the king can enter the Temple; to enter the Temple, all obstacles in the external world must be overcome," writes John Anthony West.[2]

While displayed at many of Ramesses II's temples throughout Egypt, there happen to be interesting parallels between the legend of Kadesh and the overall theme of Luxor Temple: Amun, the invisible force which permeates through all of creation, inhabits the body of the pharaoh, a representation of the Perfected Man.

THE OBELISK

Let's not step inside just yet, as there's plenty more to see outside. Just in front of the pylon is a towering obelisk, which represents man's link with the cosmos. The Egyptians called these obelisks "Tekhenu," which means "to pierce," as in "pierce the sky." Additionally, similar to pyramids, these objects likely represented the primordial mound at the beginning of creation.

These amazing monoliths were shaped from single blocks of granite from Aswan before being meticulously carved and shipped down the river. This particular obelisk once had a twin, which now stands at the Place de la Concorde in Paris.

When it was moved in 1836, the name of Ramesses II was discovered beneath the base. The remaining obelisk, meanwhile, features multiple royal names of Ramesses written in three vertical rows along each side. The titles include: The Horus, Mighty Bull, Exalter of Thebes, Favorite of the Two Goddesses, Golden Horus, King of Upper and Lower Egypt, Usermare and Chosen of Ra.

Throughout his reign, Ramesses II would commonly usurp objects created by his predecessors, but the true origins of Luxor Temple's obelisks remain unclear.

Also notice the set of four baboons at the remaining obelisk's base. According to Schwaller, the number four represents the material, or the physical matrix of all sensuous experiences. Interestingly, baboons are known to howl at the sun each morning, as if to greet the newborn sun that materializes each day.

Baboons were closely associated with the god Djehuty, better known as Thoth, a Greek corruption of the name (fig. 31). Djehuty himself was correlated with the moon. And just as the moon reflects the light of the sun, baboons seemingly salute the solar principle as they howl each sunrise.

From closer observation of the obelisks, we can see that there were actually two sets of baboons on each side, giving us a total number of eight. Interestingly enough, eight was the number of

Fig. 19. Luxor Temple's surviving obelisk

Fig. 20. Baboons at the base of the obelisk

Djehuty, the ancient Egyptian cosmic principle of wisdom, while the number also represented the manifested world and its mysteries. According to the ancient Egyptians, it was Djehuty who gave man language, writing and magic, thus giving him access to understanding these mysteries.

An ancient Egyptian text related to Djehuty and the mysteries of Hermopolis (the city of which he was patron) declares: "I am One, who becomes Two, who becomes Four, who becomes Eight, and then I am One again."[2]

Peculiarly, the east and west faces of each of Luxor Temple's obelisks are slightly convex - the reasons for which are still unknown. Another mystery is that, like all obelisk pairings in Egypt, the two obelisks here were carved at different heights. As the Egyptians were masters at precision, this was surely deliberate. But the absence of any original obelisk pairings in Upper Egypt prevents us from closer examination.

Schwaller de Lubicz's stepdaughter, Lucie Lamy, theorized that the height of the obelisks correlated to the longitude and latitude of the temple. John Anthony West, meanwhile, theorized that the obelisks served as tuning forks, as granite is a highly resonant stone.

THE COLOSSI

Lined up in front of the pylon, one can't miss the series of large colossi representing the pharaoh. Notice the sculpture to the right of the entrance that was damaged by an ancient earthquake - likely the one that occurred in 27 BC.

While Ramesses II was long gone by that point, the symbolic function of his statues remained relevant. Here we can see that the statue was cracked right through yet still survived largely intact. In the parts with the cracks, espe-

Fig. 21. A cross-armed pharaoh placed outside in modern times

cially on the lefthand side of the base, notice how mortices have been cut to rejoin the cracked sections.

Considering how the ancient Egyptians regarded sacred art, symbols and entire temples as living organisms that were capable of withholding and transmuting potent spiritual energy, it's possible that these mortices were largely symbolic.

Fig. 22. A seated colossal statue of Ramesses II

Instead of fixing the sculpture either aesthetically or structurally, they may have mainly served as "energetic bandaids" of sorts.

Another peculiarity is the colossi all the way to the left (east). Unlike the other striding and seated statues, here the pharaoh is standing upright with his arms crossed like Osiris (fig. 21). What's more, is that its eyes and other facial features don't match those of the other statues. This colossi, in fact, was only placed here in recent times.

We know this because a relief inside the Court of Ramesses II (fig. 36) reveals how Luxor Temple's facade looked during the 19th Dynasty, and no statue with an Osirian pose was included. The piece was, however, dug up in front of the pylon before being reburied in the 20th century to keep it preserved. Later on, it was pieced together and placed here during recent restoration of the pylon.

But where was it originally? Most likely, it was placed near the eastern portal (also known as the *dwa rekhyt* entrance) of the Court of Ramesses II. Its twin probably remains buried to this day.

AROUND THE FORECOURT

Also around the forecourt are the remains of various structures built by the Late Period pharaohs. During the 25th Dynasty (747-656 BC), Pharaoh Shabaka would build a kiosk here while Taharqa would add a Hathor chapel. While both are in ruins, some remnants of the chapel can be seen to the west.

In better condition is a small Roman chapel built during the reign of Hadrian which still contains a statue of Isis. Also in the area are the foundations of a Christian church, likely for the veneration of St. Mary.

Another curious artifact in the forecourt is a stele dating to the first regnal year of Thutmosis IV (r. 1397–1388 BC). Now on display near Hadrian's Isis temple, it was originally placed in front of the east pylon. This is especially curious considering that Thutmosis IV was Amenhotep III's father, and the pylon wasn't even built until the reign of Ramesses II. A hieroglyphic inscription, however, reveals that the stele was restored at some point by Seti I, Ramesses' father.

The headless statue next to the stele, meanwhile, was long believed to have been created by Merenptah (the son of Ramesses II), with a carving on the side representing his mother. The statue, however, was likely usurped, as the style of its collar bone is the same as those created by Amenhotep III.

In regards to the pylon entrance, by Ramesses II's reign, it was no longer used during the annual Opet Festival, as the journey would take place on boat instead. It was likely used, however, as part of another important ceremony.

During the ninth month of the Egyptian calendar known as Pashons (which corresponds to 9 May – 7 June), a procession involving the ithyphallic statue of Min-Amun would walk through this gate. It marked the beginning of the Peret season, when the land was plowed following the inundation of the Nile River. The king would traditionally cut the first crop, symbolizing the cutting of Egypt's enemies as well as his role as provider for his people.

We'll be seeing a lot of this specific form of Amun throughout the temple (fig. 44), while his image is also ubiquitous throughout other temples like Karnak. In short, Min-Amun represented the universal creative force manifest as sexuality.

It's now finally time to step inside the temple, beginning a journey that only a select few would've had the privilege of experiencing in the age of the pharaohs.

THE COURT OF RAMESSES II

Looking at the temple map, one of the first things that stands out is the skewed axis of the Court of Ramesses II. Some believe it was built this way to align Luxor Temple with Karnak.

Others, meanwhile, believe it was deliberately skewed in response to the curve of the Nile.

Still, other scholars claim that, given the long gap between the two main phases of Luxor Temple's construction, the axis had to be adjusted in accordance with shifting astronomical alignments.

Schwaller de Lubicz, on the other hand, argued that the plan was firmly in place since the time of Amenhotep, son of Hapu. But what did this unusual temple layout signify? Walking through the court, you'll encounter multiple colossal statues of Ramesses II mid-stride, which provides us with a big hint.

When an outline of one of these statues is superimposed over the temple map, we see that not only does this portion of the temple represent the legs from the knee down, but the action of man taking a step (fig. 4).

Nature and the cosmos are constantly in motion, and these forces are also present within man. Rather than sitting around idly, it's human destiny to take a step forward in hopes of achieving a greater goal.

Fig. 23. The striding statues of the Court of Ramesses II

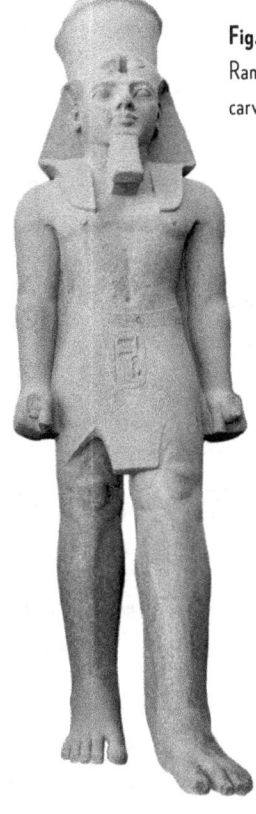

Fig. 24. A colossal Ramesses statue carved to perfection

Notice how each statue is striding with its left foot forward. But why left? It's because the heart is on the left side of the body. In contrast to modern scientific reasoning with its emphasis on the brain, the Egyptians believed the heart to be the true seat of consciousness.

Symbolism aside, one can't help but marvel at the granite statues of Ramesses II here at Luxor Temple and elsewhere around Egypt. Not only is granite one of the hardest stones, but the master sculptors were able to create almost perfectly symmetrical statues - and in great quantity, too.

Engineer Christopher Dunn was astonished by these colossal statues when first visiting Luxor Temple on a tour led by John Anthony West. Carefully examining and measuring multiple still photographs of the sculptures and their crowns, he concluded that the extreme level of precision with which they were made would be extremely difficult to pull off even today.

Aside from the monumental statues, the court is surrounded by double-rows of papyrus bud columns which add up to 74 in total. And at 57 meters deep by 50.9 meters wide, this is one of the largest individual sections of Luxor Temple.

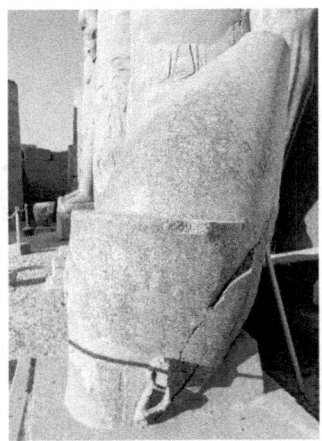

Fig. 25. A fallen crown

Fig. 26. The Shrine of Hatshepsut

The court, in fact, could be considered its own temple within a temple. It was officially titled "The Temple of Ramesses Meriamun United with Eternity," a name to later be reused by Ramesses III at his mortuary temple at Medinet Habu .

Back near the court entrance, don't miss the Shrine of Hatshepsut. As mentioned earlier, Hatshepsut and her co-regent Thutmosis III constructed a way station in this area before the reign of Amenhotep III. It was here that the solar barques and statues of the Theban Triad (Amun, Mut and Khonsu) would be cleansed during the annual Opet Festival.

At first glance, nothing about this way station appears out of the ordinary. But when examining a map of the temple, we can see that if a straight line is drawn from the Central Barque Shrine, it directly connects to this way station's back wall! (Remarkably, this is in spite of the skewed axis.) One wonders, then, if the original plan for Luxor Temple had been known even prior to the reign of

Fig. 27. Abu el-Haggag Mosque

Amenhotep III (see p91 for more information on the temple axes and p112 for more on Luxor Temple's potential hidden origins).

Another anomaly in the Court of Ramesses II is a much more recent one: the Abu el-Haggag Mosque. The Romans first built a fortress here in the 4th century AD, over which the Copts built a church in the 6th century. Later filled in, the former church then served as a platform for a new mosque which has remained in constant use ever since.

Notice how it stands at about eight meters above the current ground level. This provides us with a clear image of how much sand filled the temple when Napoleon and his troops arrived in Egypt in the late 18th century.

Archaeologists have previously attempted to get the mosque removed in an effort to fully excavate and research the temple, as it blocks numerous fine reliefs on the eastern wall of the Court of Ramesses II. While their requests were denied and the mosque

Fig. 28. Ancient Egyptian columns emerging through the floor of the mosque

remains in place, its main entrance shifted to the east in the 1960s. Interestingly, the original entrance can still be observed when looking up from the court's entryway.

If you get the chance to visit the mosque, you'll observe how many of the original columns jut out of the modern flooring and are still connected by their hieroglyph-inscribed architraves (fig. 28).

As incongruous as it may appear today, Abu el-Haggag's existence means that Luxor Temple has been in constant use as a religious site, in some form or another, for over three millennia!

On your way out of the court, you'll encounter two seated colossi of Ramesses II on either side of the exit. Note the small figure of the pharaoh's beloved queen, Nefertari, who's nestled beside her husband's right leg. On the other side of the river in the Valley of the Queens, her vivid tomb is among the most beautiful ever discovered in Egypt.

It's this precise spot, according to the temple plan, that corresponds to the knees. If the seated statues weren't enough of a giveaway, take note of the reliefs carved into the side of each base.

The scene, which depicts a mirror image of Hapi, the Nile River god, is a common one throughout Egypt (fig. 38). But notice how the gap in the stone runs precisely through Hapi's knees! According to Schwaller de Lubicz, the Egyptians were so meticulous that even things like stone gaps were carefully and deliberately planned.

THE RELIEFS IN DETAIL

THE EASTERN PORTAL

Over to the court's east, you'll find a portal that was known to the ancient Egyptians as *dwa rekhyt*. It was named after the Rekhyt (lapwing) bird, which was used as a symbol to depict the common people in Egyptian society, or possibly foreigners. As such, the gate's name could be translated as "The Gate From Which the Plebeians (or Foreigners) Adore."

From an esoteric perspective, the Rekhyt may have represented the uninitiated. In any case, the symbol at this spot likely indicated that commoners (or foreigners, or the uninitiated) could step no further into the temple beyond this point.

Certain parts of Egyptian temples were restricted to certain individuals based on their initiatory degree. It's

Fig. 29. A Rekhyt bird

possible, however, that commoners were granted closer access than usual during certain festivals – but never *too* close.

At some Egyptian temples, certain inscriptions declare that those who were sick, insane, unclean or simply uninitiated, were not allowed to enter. Later in the Ptolemaic era, when Egypt was ruled by descendants of Alexander the Great's general, a text at Dendera even declares that "no Asiatic shall enter it, no Greek shall walk in it." As we can see, the Egyptians felt strongly that the presence of an outsider could potentially diminish the sanctity of a sacred space.

Taking a closer look at the Rekhyt bird, a symbol you will find all over Egypt, notice how the figure is depicted on what appears to be a lapwing bird's nest (fig. 29). Interestingly, in this context, this shape also represents the Egyptian hieroglyph *neb*, meaning "all," implying that the bird represents "all of the people." Accordingly, the upraised arms of the bird represent the commoners' adoration for the pharaoh, while the pinned back wings represent their acquiescence.

In front of the bird, take note of the five-pointed star, which also means to "worship" or "adore," or in some contexts, "connect."

THE EASTERN WALL, SOUTH OF THE GATE

To the south of the portal is a series of reliefs that are largely cultic in theme. In the left of the central register, we see Ramesses II offering incense to Amun as well as his own *ka* (one's life force that was often depicted as a body double). Invocations and offerings are then made to Amun, also known as the "Invisible One," and his various attributes.

Beneath it is a frieze depicting a procession of the personifications of different resource-rich regions of the world. These include, from left to right, Djahi (the Levantine Coast), the Central Islands, Keftiu (likely Crete), Sangar (Babylon), Kheta (the Anatolian Hittite Empire), Alasa (Cyprus), the "Land of the Cows," Kenmut (the land between the Siwa Oasis and Kharaga Oasis), Land of the Neters (possibly the Red Sea Coast or near the straits of Bab el Mandeb), Coptos, Edfu, and several other locations. Some of the hieroglyphs in between the above-mentioned names are now illegible. The relief also shows how the various mines and quarries of the Egyptian Empire contributed to the temple.

Fig. 30. Seshat, the goddess of writing

Above the frieze is a band of text which reads: "Ramesses, beloved of the King of the Gods Amun, Lord of Heaven, the Ruler of Waset (Ancient Thebes), made it as his monument for his father Amun-Ra, Lord of the Thrones of the Two Lands, making for him a temple with doors and flagstones being of cedar from Lebanon fitted with Asiatic copper. All the cult images full of life, power and health are made of diorite and granite."

THE SOUTH WALL

The theme continues on the facade of the south wall, immediately to the left of the original gate of the 18th Dynasty. Here we see Ramesses II making various offerings to the many gods residing in the temple. The king is accompanied by a retinue of *neteru*, the last and best-preserved of which is Seshat, the goddess of writing.

Also known as the Mistress of the House of Books, she's shown here writing upon a frond, or leaf of a palm. Here she predicts a

Fig. 31. Djehuty, the god of wisdom and writing

long and prosperous reign for the pharaoh consisting of many years and many jubilees (fig. 30).

Notice the insignia above her head, which has never been fully identified. Some Egyptologists have labeled it as a rosette, while others see it as a cannabis plant. Others, meanwhile, see it as a star. The fact that it's covered by some sort of canopy further adds to the enigma.

The facade also shows a large scene of Ramesses II offering an image of Maat to Amun with his consort Mut behind him. Maat, both a goddess and a general concept, represents cosmic harmony and the natural order of the universe.

Ancient Egyptian society, like many traditional cultures, was based on the idea that the social order should reflect cosmic principles. The organization of society into a particular structure, as well as the performance of specific rituals, were vital to maintaining the delicate balance between humanity and natural law. The concept of Maat is analogous to that of *dharma* found in Eastern philosophies like Hinduism and Buddhism.

It was the pharaoh's responsibility to uphold Maat during his reign, and throughout Egypt we commonly see reliefs of the king presenting a statuette of the goddess to deities like Amun. Actual rituals like this probably took place in the early mornings to assure the gods that nothing had occurred throughout the night to disrupt the natural order.

At the top of the gate we see a scene showing a ritual of legitimization of the king's reign (fig. 32). Here Ramesses is sitting in

Fig. 32. Djehuty, Ramesses and the ished tree

an ished tree which once stood in the Great Sun Temple of Heliopolis (north of modern-day Cairo). According to Egyptian mythology, the tree would mysteriously produce the name of the king-to-be on its leaves in glyphs of gold or silver. This was said to have miraculously occurred on the eve of the new pharaoh's succession.

We also see the ibis-headed Djehuty, a personification of the principle of wisdom and writing. He's shown carrying a palm frond and, similar to the relief of Seshat mentioned earlier, promises a long and prosperous reign. Notably, we can see a much larger version of this type of scene on the wall of Ramesses II's mortuary temple, the Ramesseum, located on the other side of the river.

Likely native to Nubia and Ethiopia, the ished tree was probably imported to Egypt and is believed by some to have been an acacia tree. The acacia tree has the ability to thrive in the barren desert, even through long periods of drought. Not only does it provide shade for both people and animals, but its leaves and seeds are edible. From the symbolist perspective, the ished/acacia represents protection and resilience. Accordingly, the Egyptians associated it with the Tree of Life.

Interestingly, in the Freemasonic tradition, the master mason Hiram Abif, who designed the Temple of Solomon in Jerusalem, had his burial place marked by an acacia branch. The tree has long been used in Masonic funerals to represent both initiation and rebirth, with death being considered the greatest initiation of them all.

Schwaller de Lubicz, on the other hand, believed the ished tree to be a persea tree, a species native to Egypt on which avocados grow. He suggested that by wrapping linen around the fruit's pit, letters could be traced with a stylus, exuding a special type of permanent ink. And with this ink, a king's name could be written for all eternity.

Another potential contender, meanwhile, is the Cordia myxa, a medium-sized tree that grows in Lebanon and Syria. Its fruit exudes a pulp that may have been used in the creation of papyrus sheets, an object closely associated with Djehuty, the god of knowledge and writing.

This depiction of the ished tree is one of two found at Luxor Temple, with the other being in the Hall of Twelve Columns at the temple's opposite end. Fascinatingly, this relief shows a pharaoh on his knees at the part of the temple which corresponds to the knees, while the other tree can be found at the section which corresponds to the pituitary gland, a gland responsible for growth. According to Schwaller, this could not have been a coincidence.

At the bottom of the wall, see if you can locate a lightly incised relief of the high priest Pinedjim of the 21st Dynasty worshiping an effaced image of a god, likely Amun. By this time, the prosperous New Kingdom era had ended, with political power shifting north to Tanis in the Nile Delta. Luxor had become impoverished and was largely controlled by the priesthood of Amun. With no funds available for additions to Luxor Temple, this single relief is evidence of the sorry state of affairs in this area during the 21st Dynasty (1069-945 BC).

THE WESTERN WALL, NORTH OF THE PORTAL

The reliefs on the northern half of the western wall are meant to be read left to right. We first see Ramesses II as a royal celebrant in the presence of Amun in both his standard and ithyphallic forms. Here the king offers sacrificial cattle to Amun and his consort.

Moving left to right (or south to north), we then see the pharaoh depicted driving four calves before the ithyphallic Min-Amun. As mentioned, the number four is closely related to the manifestation of our physical universe, a topic we'll touch more on as we proceed deeper into the temple.

Min-Amun is also referred to as Amun-Kamutef, or "Amun Bull-of-His-Mother." The bull is a universal symbol of sexual prowess and virility, while a mother represents fertility. As mentioned earlier, Min-Amun represents the forces of creation manifest as sexual energy. Appropriately, here we see lettuce leaves growing behind the god, which were considered sacred to Min-Amun and used by the ancient Egyptians as an aphrodisiac.

Fig. 33. A depiction of the shnt pole ritual

Next we see Ramesses II adorning the red crown, a symbol of Lower Egypt. He strikes a set of chests before Amun. These chests, transliterated as *mrt*, possibly contained fabric, and the pharaoh would break them open during particular rituals. *Mrt* boxes were items closely associated with Neith, the goddess of weaving, who, on a metaphysical level, represented the invisible matrix.

Again, we see four, the number of physical materialization. The four boxes sit on four sledges, with four feathers, a symbol of the primordial god Shu, emerging from each (see p68 for more information on the mysterious *mrt* boxes).

We then see Ramesses wearing the white crown of Upper Egypt performing a ceremonial race while carrying vases in his hand. (Appropriately, these racing scenes are located in the part of the temple correlated with man taking a step.) Yet again, the pharaoh is in front of Min-Amun. This was a common rite in many ancient Egyptian ceremonies, particularly jubilee celebrations. Finally, we see Ramesses II making an offering to Amun and his consort Mut.

Generally speaking, sacrifices and offerings correspond to the never-ending cycle of destruction and creation that takes place throughout our universe. Additionally, such rites typically took place during consecration rituals.

While Luxor Temple had long been active by the reign of Ramesses II, as mentioned earlier, this court was thought of as its own temple. Thus, in this section dedicated to the lower leg, such consecration scenes are intended to "kick things off." As we'll go over later, many of the scenes here mirror those in the Hypostyle Hall, the section related to the consecration of the first phase of the temple built by Amenhotep III.

The final scene here involves the ritual of the erection of the *shnt* pole, a rite that was part of the annual Festival of Min, which itself was likely related to consecration rites. This happens to be one of the best examples of such a scene in all of Luxor (fig. 33).

Here we see the king wearing the Pschent crown (the double crown of Upper and Lower Egypt) standing before Min-Amun. In his left (receptive) hand, he holds an Ankh, a symbol of enduring life, while in his raised right (active) hand he holds a scepter. He raises it in front of the *shnt* pole and Min-Amun, as nearby priests wearing Libyan-style feathers in their hair help keep the pole stable.

Before leaving this part of the wall, there's a particular relief of Amun you should try looking for towards the far north, opposite the Shrine of

Fig. 34. A missing stone in Amun's lower leg

Hatshepsut. At first glance, it's a typical depiction of Amun wearing his plumed headdress and holding a staff. But looking closely at his lower leg, you should notice a small piece of missing stone (fig. 34).

It can be quite hard to spot at first, as people have more recently carved several dovecotes into the wall, while other parts of the relief are slightly damaged. But according to Schwaller, a piece of stone has been missing from Amun's lower leg since ancient Egyptian times.

Is it a coincidence that a stone here is missing in the precise portion of the temple related to the lower leg? Schwaller certainly didn't think so. In fact, he found over a dozen reliefs throughout the temple with missing stones. And amazingly, the locations of the gaps match almost perfectly with the body part to which that specific hall corresponds! (To be fair, there do seem to be several that don't completely match, though many of them do.)

This is one of the most obvious signs the builders of Luxor Temple left behind in regards to the temple's correspondence to the human form. We'll be covering additional examples of this phenomenon in later sections.

THE WESTERN WALL (SOUTH OF THE PORTAL) & THE SOUTH WALL

Over to the left (south) of the western wall's portal is a separate set of scenes meant to be read from right to left. Here we see the daughters of Ramesses II, followed by scenes of people bringing in livestock, including fattened oxen who were commonly sacrificed during rituals. The oxen have been so fattened, in fact, that they have a difficult time walking. Their hides have been branded with an iron, while the animals have been adorned with garlands (fig. 35).

Notice how two of the oxen have contoured horns which seem to resemble human arms, while a head has been added so that they represent an Asiatic or an African. This appears to be an example of the Egyptians using sympathetic magic, or a magical ritual involving a depiction of the intended target. In addition to the Nine Bows depicted on the pylon, the Egyptians had many other ways of representing conquest over their enemies.

Fig. 35. Fattened oxen, in this instance representing Egypt's enemies

This same set of scenes ultimately wraps around to the southern wall, where we see the 17 sons of Ramesses leading a group of bulls for sacrifice, ordered from oldest to youngest. The 13th son in line is Merenptah, who would succeed the aged Ramesses II when the 12th-oldest brother died prematurely. Each son is accompanied by his name and official titles. What's more, is that the hieroglyphs also include a complete list of officials during Ramesses II's reign.

What follows are some interesting reliefs depicting the outer pylon, complete with the obelisks and colossi we see today (fig. 36). The four flags mentioned earlier can be seen as well, giving us a fascinating glimpse into what one could've expected to see here a few thousand years ago. Interestingly, while the colossi are depicted as well, they're seen facing one another rather than forward.

Fig. 36. The outer pylon as seen in the 19th Dynasty, as depicted on the court's south wall

THE SEATED STATUES

Returning to the seated statues of Ramesses, notice how their base and sides are adorned with numerous reliefs and hieroglyphs. As mentioned earlier, the sides of each colossi's base feature a common scene of the androgynous Hapi (fig. 38).

The scene is known as *sema tawy*, or "Unification of the Two Lands," in reference to Upper and Lower Egypt. But it also contains anatomical symbolism, as it depicts the trachea (the tube connecting the voice box with the bronchi), a symbol of unification. Notice how the trachea is entwined with the papyrus and lotus plants which represent Lower and Upper Egypt, respectively.

On the front of each base is a figure of *iwn mwt ef*, meaning "Pillar of His Mother," a priest of Horus. As he gesticulates toward the king's royal cartouches, he intones a sacred formula.

On the base of the eastern colossus, you'll find carvings of captives bound by their torsos. Asiatics are depicted on the western side of the colossus and Nubians on the eastern one. You'll also find the names of various foreign lands, likely those that were dominated by Ramesses II during his reign.

The list includes the lands of Naharin (the land between the Orontes and Euphrates rivers, or modern-day Iraq), Takhsi (Damascus), Sangar (Babylon), Mittani (eastern Syria and northern Iraq), Lullu (parts of modern Iraqi Kurdistan and present Iran), Assyria, Pabekh (Armenia), Shasu (the Bedouins) and various names of places in Nubia.

Notably, Ramesses II had never made it as far as Iraq, though Thutmosis

Fig. 37. A seated colossi

III had during the 18th Dynasty. It would appear, then, that Ramesses II was paying homage to the time when the Egyptian Empire was at its peak.

On the back of each colossus are deeply carved inscriptions listing the names and titles of Ramesses II. And on the western colossus, we see a scene similar to that of the south wall, in which Djehuty and his consort Seshat write down the name of the king on the "Palms of Millions of Years." As evidenced by these carvings, some of Ramesses II's most beautiful reliefs were carved early on in his reign.

On the wall opposing this scene, which is the west door jamb of the portal, you'll find a relief of Amenhotep III presenting an offering to Amun in the presence of Mut in leonine form. While the scene has been left in place since the 18th Dynasty, the image of Amun was chiseled out during the reign of Amenhotep's son, Akhenaten. This was Akhenaten's sole contribution to the Colonnade that we will now enter.

Fig. 38. A relief of Hapi the river god, symbolizing the unification of Upper and Lower Egypt

THE COLONNADE

········ ⚱ ········

Fig. 39. The 14 columns of the Colonnade

The long Colonnade is the last section to have been finished during the 18th Dynasty. Stepping inside, you'll encounter two sets of seated statues depicting a pharaoh and his queen (fig. 40). Many believe them to be Amenhotep III and Queen Tiy, one of the most influential couples in Egyptian history.

Others, meanwhile, believe them to represent Tutankhamun and his wife Ankesenamun. But it's hard to know for sure, as many of Tut's cartouches were later appropriated by Horemheb and then Ramesses. Regardless of which historical figures they represent, the royal couple here is identified with Amun and his consort Mut (or possibly Amunet, as we'll cover shortly).

As with many ancient Egyptian statues, their noses were deliberately damaged. The Egyptians believed that things like stone statues could become infused with spirit and were therefore "alive." And while the reasons for doing so likely varied, smashing a statue's nose, thus removing its "breath of life," was the quickest way to put it out of commission.

But here we have a unique case of an attempted "resuscitation." Archaeological evidence suggests that the Mut statue was restored in Roman times. But later on, the collapse of the Colonnade's roof

Fig. 40. Statues of the pharaoh and his consort at the Colonnade's entrance

smashed her face yet again. The original Roman-era pieces were then rediscovered in the 1990s by researchers from the University of Chicago, and they'd go on to fix the face in 1997. Now, for the first time in millennia, the statue's face is mostly complete.

As discussed earlier, Amun, the primary deity worshipped by the Egyptians throughout the New Kingdom period, represents the invisible force of creation and the animating spirit that permeates all living creatures. In Egyptian mythology, Amun had two consorts, one of whom was Mut, whose name means "mother" in the Egyptian language.

Hieroglyphically, Mut is represented as a vulture, itself a symbol of virgin birth. This was likely because vultures are not sexually dimorphic, or in other words, males and females cannot be distinguished at a glance. Therefore, it appeared to the Egyptians that all vultures were female who reproduced through an endless series of virgin births.

What's more, is that vultures largely feed on dead animals, reminding us of the endless cycle of death and rebirth. Throughout

Egyptian history, various queens would wear vulture crowns which also symbolized the goddess Nekhbet, patroness of Upper Egypt.

In Egyptian mythology, Amun and Mut had a child named Khonsu. Despite being male, Khonsu represented concepts like fertility and lunar cycles. And together, all three gods formed what's known as the Theban Triad.

Amunet, on the other hand, was Amun's original mythological consort. She shares many characteristics in common with Amun, making her the feminine aspect of the same principles. The pair was one of four couples worshiped as primordial deities in the creation myths of Hermopolis. Notably, Tutankhamun erected a large statue of Amunet at Karnak during his reign.

On the pairs of statues, notice how the queen's (or Mut's, or Amunet's) hand supports her husband's back and shoulder, almost as if she is presenting him to the world. It reminds us of the adage "behind every good man is a great woman." And metaphysically speaking, it is indeed the divine feminine principle that's behind every human birth - not to mention our physical reality as a whole.

Looking ahead, you'll notice that the Colonnade consists of two rows of seven columns each. But why seven? According to John Anthony West, "Whenever there is an emphasis upon the number seven, we may look for symbolism reflecting in some way the principles of growth, process, the undying cyclical aspect of the universe."[3] Accordingly, a musical scale contains seven notes before repeating itself on a higher octave.

Given this section's emphasis on cycles, it's fitting that the reliefs depict the Opet Festival which commemorated the annual Nile flood. For thousands of years, Egypt, a country that sees little rain, relied on the flooding of the Nile for agriculture. The waters, which carried rich volcanic silt, turned the land along the river black. This is why the Egyptians called their country Kemet, or the "Black Land."

Sadly, the reliefs here are both faint and largely damaged, making them difficult to make out at any time of day. But if you put forth the effort, you can still discern some of the scenes.

Things begin on the western wall, with the first scenes taking place at Karnak. Preparations for the procession are made as girls dance. The solar barques of Amun, Mut and Khonsu are then brought to Luxor Temple by boat. Sacrifices and offerings to the gods are made as acrobats perform. The east side, meanwhile, depicts the return of the statues to Karnak, where even more sacrifices and festivities take place. Thus the cycle is complete.

As mentioned earlier, the first part of this procession originally took place on land. But by the time this Colonnade was constructed, the roundtrip journey took place on water. And in contrast to the earlier reliefs on Hatshepsut's Red Chapel, here we see all three members of the Theban Triad instead of just the solar barque of Amun.

Anatomically speaking, the Colonnade corresponds to the femur. This is fitting given the theme of cycles and motions represented both numerically and in the reliefs. Not only does the shape

Fig. 41. Offerings for the Opet Festival

of the Colonnade resemble a femur, but without our thighs, we're totally immobile.

The bone marrow of the femur is also responsible for producing many of the body's red blood cells, thus providing it with nourishment. It's appropriate, then, that the Colonnade's reliefs portray a feast.

THE ARTWORK OF THE COLONNADE

During your walk through the Colonnade, take note of the unique artistic style of the reliefs, most of which were added during the reign of Tutankhamun. But before that came the reign of Amenhotep III's son, Akhenaten.

Akhenaten would not carry on with Luxor Temple's original plans during his reign. His most notable construction in Luxor as a whole was a sanctuary called *rwd-mnw-n-iten-r-neheh* ("Sturdy are the Monuments of the Sun-Disc Forever") to the east of Karnak. It was eventually demolished by Horemheb, and Ramesses II would even use some of its blocks in Luxor Temple's pylon.

Akhenaten's agents also effaced Luxor Temple's depictions of Amun, as they would do at numerous temples throughout Egypt. And according to Schwaller de Lubicz, Akhenaten even had the names of other gods at Luxor Temple hammered out as well, only leaving the name of Atum, the ancient creator deity of Heliopolis, intact.

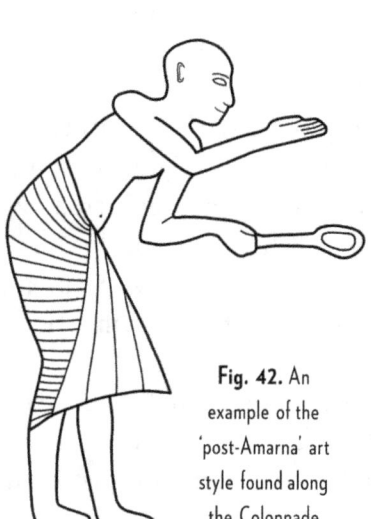

Fig. 42. An example of the 'post-Amarna' art style found along the Colonnade

While the true reasons for Akhenaten's beef with Amun remain a mystery, his longstanding feud with the priesthood of Amun at Karnak likely played a part.

As mentioned earlier, his most radical change was his alteration of the traditional Egyptian art style – something that had never been done before. Not only did Akhenaten change the art's proportions, but his artists began drawing figures in a much more dynamic and fluid style. Also, for the first time, he introduced intimate scenes of the royal family's daily life.

Bizarrely, however, instead of the ideal male form that pharaohs were typically depicted with, Akhenaten commanded his artists to draw him with an elongated face, fleshy belly and large buttocks, making him appear strikingly feminine. We now call the distinct art style from this era "Amarna art."

It wasn't long, however, before his successor, Tutankhamun, brought back the old style. But things still hadn't gone completely back to normal. Figures were still being drawn with the paunches and short legs of the Amarna style, while scenes maintained a fluid and more realistic feel compared to the art of generations past.

And this "post-Amarna art" style, as some scholars call it, is what can be seen along Luxor Temple's Colonnade. It was here that Tutankhamun carried on where twin brothers Her and Suty, the artisans of Amenhotep III and "Overseers of Works of Amun in Thebes," had left off.

Further additions were later made by Seti I, the father of Ramesses II, who fully restored Egyptian art to its original proportions and aesthetic. It could be argued, however, that his incredibly detailed artwork was more naturalistic than that of his pre-Amarna predecessors, meaning that he was in some ways still influenced by Amarna art. Some of his reliefs can be found at the south end of the hall.

Next would come Ramesses II, who, in addition to building the court and pylon, added new hieroglyphic inscriptions along the Colonnade's walls. Notice how their deep incisions contrast with the finely carved reliefs.

THE PERISTYLE COURT

Entering the Peristyle Court, the largest single portion of the temple, notice the slight ascent. Each section of the temple beyond this point was built on a *socle*, a low stone platform symbolizing the primeval mound of creation.

Stepping inside, you'll find the spacious court to be surrounded on all sides by double rows of papyrus columns. Interestingly, the court is slightly wider in the front than it is in the back, enhancing its sense of depth for those who enter.

This single area represents a multitude of body parts, including the reproductive organs, belly button, digestive tract and spine.

As discussed earlier, Schwaller de Lubicz, through years of taking meticulous measurements, discovered that the temple's proportions align accurately with a human body. Now recall the image

Fig. 43. A view of the Peristyle Court

of a striding pharaoh, as viewed from the side, superimposed over the temple plan (fig. 4). While Schwaller knew exactly where the navel was supposed to be, it would be hard to convince people - including himself - of his hypothesis should there not be something significant at this precise spot.

As you'll notice, the architraves above the columns are inscribed with hieroglyphic writing. And so Lucie Lamy, Schwaller's step-daughter who worked alongside him for years at Luxor Temple, called upon the French hieroglyphics expert Alexandre Varille.

According to Varille's translation, the inscription at the point of the navel reads: "It is here, the true site of the birth of the King, where he passed his infancy, and from whence he departed, crowned."[2]

The discovery was so astounding that Varille, a scholar trained in the "orthodox" school of academic Egyptology, would soon become a convert to Schwaller's symbolist approach. He even dedicated his first publication about Karnak to Schwaller de Lubicz.

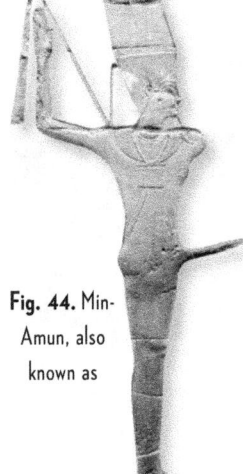

Fig. 44. Min-Amun, also known as

Tragically, he'd later die in a car accident in 1951 shortly after presenting his symbolist theories to the French Institute in Paris.

With the same side-view of the striding pharaoh in mind, Schwaller could also determine the precise location of the reproductive organs. And here on the north-facing side of the north wall we find an ithyphallic relief of Min-Amun.

As mentioned earlier, this form of Amun represents the creative urge of the universe as sexual energy. While you will indeed find Min-Amun all over the temple, his placement in this particular spot is telling. What's more, is that the temple builders left us yet another clue on the wall's opposite side.

Recall how the Court of Ramesses II, the part of the temple which corresponds to the lower leg, happens to contain a relief of Amun with a piece of stone missing in his leg. Similarly, it's on the south side of the wall here, in the spot corresponding precisely to the reproductive organs, that there's a carving of Amenhotep III with a piece of stone missing from his groin area! (It can be hard to spot, however, as the relief appears to have been recently restored, while the upper part of the pharaoh's body is also missing.)

Also on the court's south-facing north wall is an Ankh, a symbol of life, inside of which is an image of an eye, or the Egyptian hieroglyph *ir*, which means "to make" or "to cause." It's quite a fitting combination of symbols to find in this spot related to reproduction.

Over on the other side, to the west of the Colonnade, you'll find another interesting relief on the court's north-facing wall. In this spot that lines up with the wrist of a striding pharaoh, we can see a relief depicting a group of severed hands! This is a fairly common scene in Luxor, with the severed hands belonging to enemy captives. But its location here at Luxor Temple at this precise spot was surely no accident.

Yet another interesting correspondence can be found on the exterior of the western wall, which aligns with the spine. The spine, of course, is a major focal point of Eastern philosophies, as it's said to be the location of numerous chakras, or vital energy centers. Whether or not the Egyptians placed a similar emphasis on these energy centers remains up for debate. But in any case, the builders certainly utilized a creative way to represent the spine at Luxor Temple.

Viewing the wall from the outside, notice the series of thirteen charioteers that can still clearly be made out. "At precisely the spot marked by the twelfth lumbar vertebrae of the spinal column, a procession of thirteen horsedrawn chariots begins," writes John Anthony West.[3]

Fig. 45. The charioteer reliefs on the western wall's exterior

While rather confusing for those not intimately familiar with human anatomy, it's at this spot that "the cord that traverses the twelve dorsal vertebrae penetrates the first lumbar." According to Schwaller de Lubicz, the scene likely represents the formation of the physical body.

Another important discovery at the Peristyle Court was made in 1989, decades after Schwaller's research. Within a deep pit, workers found what we now call the Luxor cache, a large collection of well-preserved and exquisite statues.

The pharaohs among them include Amenhotep III, Tutankhamun and Horemheb, while the collection also featured such deities as Hathor, Atum and Horus in falcon form. As of October 1991, the collection is now on display at the Luxor Museum, an easy walk from Luxor Temple.

Much earlier in 1903, an even larger cache of statues was discovered at Karnak. But why were so many statues being buried underground at Egyptian temples? It's possibly due to practical reasons. Over the centuries, temples would become so overcrowded with statues that there simply wasn't room to house them all. The statues of the Luxor cache, it's believed, wouldn't be buried until Roman times. They must've been considered not just inconvenient, but also inappropriate when Emperor Diocletian used this precinct to station his troops.

Before moving on, note the lengthy piece of hieratic graffiti at the corner of the south wall which connects to the Hypostyle Hall, the next portion of the temple. Added by a priest during the reign of Osorkon III of the 23rd Dynasty, it tells of an incident in which a particularly high Nile flood broke the dykes and partially flooded the court.

Also note how the Hypostyle Hall rests on a slightly higher platform than that of the Peristyle Court. Observing the edge of the platform from the court reveals how its stones were recycled from older temples. While we don't know for sure, they were possibly taken from the older Middle Kingdom version of the temple that once stood here.

THE HYPOSTYLE HALL

Next, continue onward to the Hypostyle Hall, known in ancient times as "The Hall of Appearances," or *wsekhet kha'it*.

While open to the sky today, this hall, along with all of the rooms south of it, was originally covered over. But before going into detail about the hall itself, it's worth mentioning a bit about Luxor Temple's different construction phases.

The covered portion of the temple, stretching from the Triple Sanctuary to the Hypostyle Hall, could be considered the temple's first phase. And while the full temple that was finally completed by Ramesses II corresponds to the body of an adult human, Luxor Temple's covered section alone corresponds to the body of an infant.

According to the temple plan, the Hypostyle Hall aligns with the lungs and breasts of a full-grown adult. But it also aligns with the lower legs of a baby (fig. 50). Keep both of these correspondences in mind as we discuss the hall's symbolism.

Fig. 46. The Hypostyle Hall as seen from the end of the Peristyle Court

The Hypostyle Hall consists of 32 papyrus columns, some of which are inscribed with the names of later usurpers like Ramesses II, IV and VI. And while there are no direct depictions of either lungs or breasts, what we can clearly observe is lunar symbolism. Walking around the hall, pay close attention to the floor in front of each set of columns (fig. 47).

The row all the way to the back, or south, looks totally ordinary. But looking at the next row to the north, notice how a thin crescent appears before the base of each column. It grows even larger with the next row. While an even larger crescent was once visible at the fourth and final row, large blocks, presumably placed here during restorations, now obscure the view. Interestingly, similar symbolism was also utilized at the Temple of Montu in Karnak.

The lunar symbolism here is hard to deny. But what connection does it have with the human body? As John Anthony West points out, "In traditional astrology, lungs and heart are ruled by the

moon and sun respective-
ly."[3] And when one
pictures the lungs of a
living human, in a con-
stant state of inhalation
or exhalation, there are
indeed parallels with the
uninterrupted waxing and
waning of the moon.

Additionally, the walls
of the hall feature reliefs
commemorating Luxor
Temple's consecration, a
concept which could be
likened to a newborn
baby taking in its first
breath of air. From the
Rosicrucian perspective,
life begins when an
infant's first breath con-
verges with the cosmic
energy known as the
"vital life force." The
Egyptians called this force
the *ka*, and they too
believed that it fused with
a newborn's breath at the
time of birth. Further-
more, the Chinese, who

Fig. 47. The phases of the moon as carved
beside the bases of the columns

call this life force *qi*, have also long associated it with the breath.

As we discussed earlier, the ancient Egyptians regarded their
temples as living organisms. Accordingly, the reliefs in the Hypostyle
Hall, located in the section of the lungs, played an active role in
giving Luxor Temple *life*. (See the following section for more details.)

 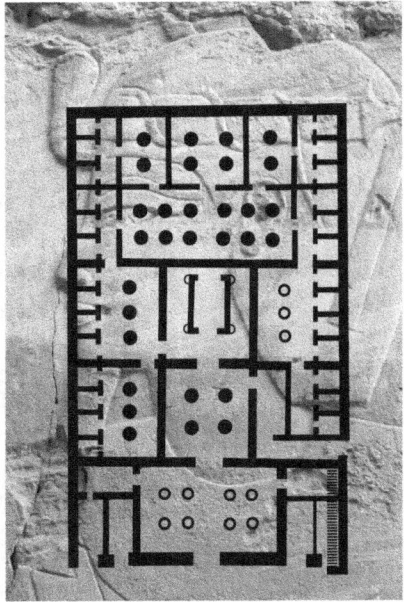

Fig. 48. A relief of the pharaoh in the Chapel of Mut

Fig. 49. The paving stones of the covered temple form a mosaic of this face

The Hypostyle Hall is also home to four additional chapels – two on the left (east) and two on the right. Of the two western chapels, one was dedicated to Amun while the other was either dedicated to a pharaoh or simply used for storage. Interestingly, the room furthest to the right likely once contained a set of stairs leading to Luxor Temple's second story. Obviously, with the roof having collapsed, nothing of these upper rooms remain.

Over on the east side are two more chapels, though the entrance to the one on the far left has been concealed with masonry. This chapel was originally dedicated to Khonsu and can still be entered via an opening on the opposite side through a room connected to the Chamber of the Divine Kings.

Of special interest to the symbolist approach to Luxor Temple is the other eastern chapel, known in Egyptology as the Chapel of Mut. On this chapel's western wall, you'll find a relief of

Amenhotep III, which appears rather ordinary at first glance (fig. 48). But this carving was of major importance to the overall temple plan.

During Schwaller de Lubicz's years of study, he noticed the irregular nature of the paving blocks throughout the covered portion of the temple. Suspecting a deliberate reason for it, he and his team went on to carefully measure every single stone.

When finished, they created a precise overhead map showing both an accurate representation of the temple structure along with the paving stones on the floor. And amazingly, when adding a bit of contrast, the stones formed a mosaic face that looks exactly like that of the carving in the Chapel of Mut! (fig. 49)

> Nothing is sensual for them; and this shocks our Western sense of aesthetics. Everything is solely didactic, of an esoteric nature; it is a teaching for the Understanding, for pure Intellect, a teaching that cannot be described in explicit terms.[1]

THE RELIEFS IN DETAIL

On the eastern wall of the main hall, we can see Amenhotep III presenting the temple to Amun and Amunet. According to the hieroglyphs, Amenhotep is "presenting the house to his lords." As mentioned earlier, these images of the temple's consecration are appropriately located in the hall which corresponds to the lungs, and therefore the temple's "first breath."

Also recall the similar reliefs added years later in the Court of Ramesses II which deal with the consecration of that "temple within a temple." As that section of Luxor Temple corresponds with an adult skeleton's lower legs, the fact that the Hypostyle Hall also corresponds with an infant's lower legs is an interesting bit of synchronicity.

In the register below, we can also see a group of deities representing the different *nomes*, or provinces of ancient Egypt. The

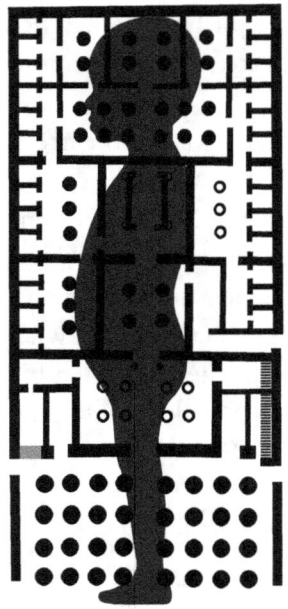

Fig. 50. An image of a baby superimposed over the closed portion of the temple

eastern wall is also decorated with scenes of the king offering things like fish, birds, milk and various ointments to Amun and Amunet.

Other reliefs include a series of vignettes spread across several registers, which again depict the king before Amun. We see the pharaoh as a celebrant in many of the same rituals we've seen Ramesses II participating in elsewhere in the temple. As these reliefs are among the temple's oldest, they surely served as inspiration for the later carvings in the Ramesses court. On that note, notice how delicate these raised reliefs are in contrast to the relatively crude and deeply incised reliefs of Ramesses II.

The reliefs of the Hypostyle Hall also reveal the wide array of crowns that a king might wear during particular ceremonies. But as we'll cover shortly, these crowns also make numerous appearances throughout the adjacent halls.

On the lower left of the wall, we see Amenhotep bringing four calves to Amun as part of a ritual. Each calf is tethered to a cord representing a cardinal direction, while the number four happens to be the number of materiality and substance. And above that, we see the king performing a libation to the same god.

Proceeding from the left part of the lower register, we then see the king smiting a set of *mrt* chests, or "boxes of cloths," before the deity (fig. 51). There are four boxes here, each originally painted a different color, which also likely represented the four cardinal directions.

As mentioned earlier, the *mrt* boxes were associated with the goddess Neith, the goddess of weaving who also represented the invisible matrix. Interestingly, the hieroglyphic symbol for Neith, which dates all the way back to the Old Kingdom, closely resembles one of these chests.

Furthermore, the rituals involving the *mrt* boxes likely date back to the Old Kingdom as well. In particular, the ritual originated as part of a festival in honor of the god Sokar (a hawk-headed deity of the underworld) during which there were four chests containing linens of different colors – green, red, white and "Egyptian blue" (*jrtjw*). The boxes were wrapped in cords and pulled by the pharaoh in an action symbolizing the unification of Egypt and its people.

As early as the Pyramid Texts, first inscribed within the 5th Dynasty pyramid tomb of Pharaoh Unas (c. 24th century BC), Neith is described as having knitted together the limbs of Osiris after Isis gathered them together. Also referred to as "Lady of the House," it is Neith who symbolized the metaphysical makeup of man. Fittingly, the *mrt* chests that represented her appear here in the portion of the temple dedicated to the lungs, man's first breath, and the temple's consecration.

Along with the four cattle to be slaughtered, the pharaoh smashes the four chests as part of a ritual, emphasizing the symbiotic relationship between destruction and creation.

Next, we see the ritual of the erection of the *shnt* pole, with the king holding it in his left hand. As mentioned in the section on the Court of Ramesses II, this ritual was associated with the Festival of Min, which in turn was likely related to consecration rituals. Here the king wears a feathered white crown known as the Atef which was associated with Osiris, Lord of the Underworld.

Over on the extreme right, the lower register shows a ritual in which the king appears with a page from a scroll as he wears the blue Khepresh, or "war crown" with a protective Uraeus in front.

The upper register on the right end depicts the king sacrificing an oryx – one of many animals who symbolized Set, who in turn represented the principle of opposition. In Egyptian mythology, the oryx was charged with trying to devour the moon. But here instead, in this room dedicated to lunar symbolism, the oryx is killed, becoming food for the moon itself.

Interestingly, Russian mystic George Gurdjieff once referred to humanity as "food for the moon" in reference to human existence being part of a vast magnetic field over which the moon governs. All things will eventually come to pass and be consumed by this magnetic field, thus becoming "food" for a new cycle of creation. This particular relief, therefore, shows the oryx, symbolic of an opposing force, being sacrificed to nourish the *ka* in this hall linked to the moon and man's first breath.

Although much of the Hypostyle Hall's southern wall has been removed, the lower register of reliefs remains intact. Here we see the personifications of Egypt's *nomes* bearing the various resources found in each district.

Notice how many of the reliefs in this portion of the temple have been effaced. Many Egyptologists believe that this was the work of Christian zealots who wanted to desecrate "pagan" iconography. But the hacking was clearly carried out carefully and deliberately.

An alternative explanation is that the ancient Egyptians themselves effaced these walls and many others throughout the country. This could've been part of an effort to "decommission" the magical properties of the reliefs. If so, it was possibly because so much time had passed that they were no longer relevant to the times, or perhaps because later priests could sense that the religion's days were numbered.

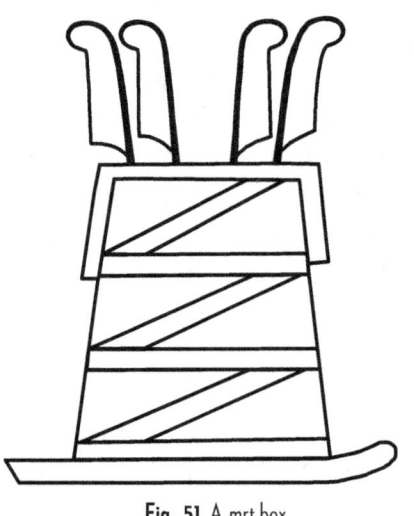

Fig. 51. A mrt box

THE CHAMBER OF THE DIVINE KINGS

········ ☥ ········

The next small portion of the temple originally contained eight columns. As you'll notice, the columns are all missing, but their bases can still be seen on the floor.

This is the part of Luxor Temple that underwent the most extensive remodeling by the Romans who later occupied the site. Interestingly, this chamber corresponds to the heart.

As mentioned earlier, the Egyptians believed the heart to be the center of consciousness. Accordingly, when it came to the mummification process, the brain was always discarded from the dead body, while the heart was left intact.

Throughout his writing, Schwaller frequently emphasizes how the symbolism or overall "sacred science" of the Egyptians cannot be understood by the rational intellect alone. Rather, a true understanding can only be achieved through the "intelligence of the heart."

With this in mind, notice the Egyptian hieroglyph on the north-facing section of the south wall which resembles a human head. This hieroglyph, read as *hr*, means "upon" or "here," and it may also be understood as "present." Interestingly, the general outline of the glyph happens to match the shape of *ib*, the hieroglyph for heart. Taking the Egyptian belief in the "intelligence of the heart" into consideration, the resemblance between these two symbols was likely no coincidence.

As for the other glyphs surrounding this particular symbol? While the arrangement of hieroglyphs here is rather unusual, the full sentence roughly translates to something like "...repeatedly upon the throne of (Horus), like Ra every day." The statement was likely related to the particular rituals that Amenhotep III performed here, on which we'll cover in more detail shortly.

The hall's original columns, as mentioned, are no more, though you will find two smaller Corinthian columns in front of the apse. These columns are made of red granite, a symbol of kingly or divine presence in ancient Rome.

And over to the left is a set of interesting reliefs dating to pre-Christian Rome. Originally thought to be early Christian imagery, the artwork depicts the original Roman Tetrarchy, in which two emperors (*Augusti*) and their subordinates (*Caesars*) ruled the two halves of the empire (fig. 53). In particular, we see emperors Diocletian (r. 284-305 AD) and Maximian (r. 286-305) along with their two junior emperors, Constantius Chlorus and Galerius. It was likely in this very hall that local Christians were once forced to pledge allegiance to these rulers.

Much of the Roman-era plaster has since peeled off the walls, revealing some of the original scenes of Amenhotep III and Amun. As we'll cover shortly, the pair is depicted together all throughout the inner shrines of the temple, but the scenes here appear to place a special emphasis on the king's crowns.

Fig. 52. The Chamber of the Divine Kings

Fig. 53. A painted depiction of the Roman Tetrarchy

To the left of the apse, we see Amenhotep kneeling before Amun as the deity touches his crown. The hieroglyphic text reads "I afix for thee thy diadem." While the multiple scenes in this set are nearly identical, the pharaoh wears a different crown in each.

For example, we see the pharaoh wearing the Atef crown, the Hemhem crown (a triple Atef) and the Pschent crown (the double crown of Upper and Lower Egypt). For whatever reason, it was deemed necessary to show the pharaoh being crowned in each for him to be considered "complete" as a ruler. Thus, these scenes relate to the legitimization of Amenhotep III's rule.

On the western section of the south wall, we can see part of a scene of Amenhotep III being suckled by a goddess. She provides him with divine nourishment, turning him into a suprahuman with the powers needed to control such an important kingdom as Egypt. Many of the other reliefs around here were apparently dismantled in the Roman era.

In pharaonic times, this section of the temple was known as the "Chamber of the Divine Kings." And it served as yet another barque shrine or way station during religious processions.

Two small rooms on either side may have served as shrines for the "Royal Barque" and the "Royal Ka." *Ka* statues represented an individual's life force and animating spirit, and they also served a practical function, acting as host to a person's actual *ka* following death.

The opening to the east leads to a room which may have once contained a staircase leading to the temple's now-lost second floor. It was likely up here that priests performed rituals involving images of the *neteru*, similar to rituals that would later take place on the roof of Dendera. This room also leads to the small Khonsu chapel in the Hypostyle Hall to which the front entrance has been concealed with masonry.

Over on the north wall, we can see some interesting reliefs which show evidence of effacement during the reign of Akhenaten. The reliefs show Amenhotep pouring libations in front of Amun. But Akhenaten even went as far as vandalizing his own father's name, as it happened to contain the name of Amun! The royal names were later recut by the Ramesside kings.

Ramesses II would also recarve many of the images of Amun that were vandalized during Akhenaten's reign. Interestingly, while Amun was typically colored in red during the 18th Dynasty, by the 19th Dynasty he became blue, and we can see faint traces of blue pigment here. Symbolically speaking, the color change may have represented Amun transitioning from a solar deity to more of a cosmic one.

Other scenes on this wall show the vulture goddess and patroness of Upper Egypt, Nekhbet. Behind the king, meanwhile, are a group of men carrying swords and shields. And in the middle register are various priests. Behind them is a large assembly of 24 men who carry the king's throne.

Interestingly, the throne, adorned with lion carvings on either side, closely resembles those that Akhenaten would use in his own jubilees. But while he liked the throne, he didn't approve of many of these reliefs, as he'd also remove an entire long inscription that had been carved above them.

Fig. 54. The apse

Continuing south to the next chamber, it should be noted that the current opening is not the original. As mentioned, the Romans converted this hall into a temple of worship for the Imperial Cult, and they were the ones to install the apse, blocking the original entrance to the next chamber. The current opening was later cut in the 1950s by the Antiquities Department.

As you continue onward, observe the block to the right which was reused from elsewhere. In addition to an image of Hapi, it contains the cartouche of Pharaoh Ay (1323–1319 BC), Akhenaten's vizier and then Tutankhamun's successor. Following his four-year rule, the Amarna period would officially come to an end.

THE OFFERING VESTIBULE

The next section of the temple still has its original roof intact, and the dim lighting of these inner shrines adds to their mystical ambiance.

The first room you'll find yourself in, known as the Offering Vestibule, is entirely decorated in ornate reliefs, some of them with their original vibrant colors intact. The numerous scenes here yet again depict Amenhotep III presenting all sorts of offerings to Amun. And we know that in pharaonic times, ritual offerings like those in the reliefs were indeed presented to the gods here.

Some scenes show Amenhotep III directing cattle to the temple where they would then be ritually sacrificed. Additional offerings include flowers, vases and incense. On the south wall, we then see Amun accepting the pharaoh's offerings, resulting in their spiritual union (see the following section for a detailed explanation).

You'll also notice how this room contains four columns. As discussed earlier, the Egyptians regarded four as the number of material, or the principle of substantiality. And in the Egyptian and Western esoteric traditions, the material world is comprised of four elements.

Fig. 55. The Offering Vestibule

But the names of these elements are merely symbolic, and not to be taken literally. The active principle is represented by Fire, the receptive principle by Earth, the mediating principle by Air and the composite of all three by Water, which acts as a fourth and distinct principle.

What's more, is that it's in this antechamber that the Axis of Amun and the Longitudinal Axis (the Axis of Khonsu) discovered by Schwaller de Lubicz transect (see p91). While not visible to the naked eye, such a transection brings to mind a cross.

On a metaphysical level, crosses symbolize both the polarities that arose out of the Primordial Scission and also the reconciliation of those polarities. Or in other words, the cross represents the Perfected Man overcoming polarities in order to achieve Unity.

THE RELIEFS IN DETAIL

All of the walls in this room feature an uppermost band depicting the cobra goddess Wadjet. Below that is another register featuring a kneeling Amenhotep III presenting various offerings to Amun. You'll then find three main registers depicting various scenes, the details of which are described below.

THE NORTH WALL

The north wall of the room saw some damage at the hands of the Romans when they installed the apse on the other side. But surrounding the opening, you can still make out the three main registers of reliefs.

In the upper register, we see the king being initiated into the ancient mysteries. And to the right, the pharaoh wears the Atef crown as he presents four cows to the ithyphallic Min-Amun.

In the middle register, the king wears the red crown of Lower Egypt as he presents numerous offerings to Amun. Or at least this is what the scene once depicted. After Akhenaten effaced the

Amun carving, later Ramesside pharaohs had the space filled in with images of priests.

This includes a depiction of the Iunmutef Priest, a special priest whose roles were to help uphold Maat, or cosmic harmony, and to ensure the king's legitimacy.

We also see the divine female consort who was known as "God's Hand," along with some offerings intended for the Queen (or at least a figure representing her). The priest then summons Amun to partake in the offerings presented by Amenhotep.

In the next register, we see the king and his *ka* observing the bovine animals about to be sacrificed. And to the right, the king wears the blue crown next to a text that reads: "As King of Upper and Lower Egypt, upon the Horus throne of the living, shall he appear for all eternity."

The reliefs above the door have been partially damaged, but we can still see fragments of the king racing. To the left of the door in the middle register, the king wears the blue Khepresh crown while pouring a libation for the trussed bulls about to be sacrificed.

The king wears the same crown in the register below in the presence of Amun along with some priests. They're all enveloped in a large blanket adorned with stars that resembles the night sky.

THE EAST WALL

The reliefs on the east wall are spread across three main registers and are meant to be looked at from left to right.

In the upper register, we see the king embraced by Amun as he offers a necklace to the deity. Next, we see the king wearing the blue crown while lighting incense for Min-Amun as the vulture goddess Nekhbet hovers above the pharaoh.

This is followed by the king in the double crown of Upper and Lower Egypt holding a scepter above a table covered in metallic offering vessels as Amun faces the king. We then see the king in the Atef crown striking the ritual *mrt* chests in the presence of Amun. And on the extreme right, we see Amenhotep III shaking sistrums of Hathor (a musical rattle used during certain religious festivals) as Amun presents him with "life," or the Ankh symbol.

On the far left of the middle register, we see a group of priests carrying a sacred barque as the king wears the white crown. The king later appears again and is seen censing before it. He does the same for the barque of Amun. Next, before Mut, the pharaoh is seen wearing the blue Khephresh crown while standing under Nekhbet, holding a crook over his right shoulder.

The lower register begins with the king wearing the Nemes headdress (yet another type of royal headgear) while presenting offerings to Amun. In the next image, he's wearing the Khephresh crown while being accompanied by his *ka*. Much of this relief is now obscured by a cavity in the wall that was created by squatters shortly after the Arab conquest. We next see the pharaoh waving his scepter over a wide variety of offerings, followed by him pouring libations over Amun and his consort.

Fig. 56. Reliefs along the Offering Vestibule's east wall

THE WEST WALL

The west wall of the chambers contains three major registers which are meant to be read from right to left.

First, on the extreme right, we see the pharaoh running with vases before Min-Amun, and to the left, he gestures over a table of offerings. Next, he gesticulates four times over the offerings in front of the ithyphallic Min-Amun. Finally, the Iunmutef Priest recites a hymn as Wadjet and Nekhbet, the patron deities of Lower and Upper Egypt, respectively, rejoice.

In the middle register, we see the pharaoh in a wig waving his scepter before priests carrying boxes of cultic objects. They exclaim: "May Mut come in peace and lavish love on Amenhotep III!" We then see the king and the priests again, bearing offerings for Amun who promises "life" and "welfare."

In the bottom register, we see the priests carrying large jars, topped with stoppers in the form of a ram, which, as we know, is a symbol of Amun. The king also carries a vase in what appears to be part of a ritual related to the coming annual Nile flood.

Fig. 57. Amun on his throne

THE SOUTH WALL

On the gate which leads to the Central Barque Shrine, we can see deities like Montu, Sekhmet and Hathor, among others, leading the pharaoh toward Amun. The Invisible One then embraces the king, permitting him into his inner sanctum (fig. 57).

While this relief of Amun was damaged by Akhenaten's iconoclast movement, it was later restored by the Ramesside kings.

THE HALL OF THEOGAMY

········ ☥ ········

Just ahead of you is the Central Barque Sanctuary, also known as the Shrine of Alexander. But first, directly to the left of the Offering Vestibule and through what is called the Coronation Room, don't miss an additional small yet extremely important hall.

Schwaller de Lubicz called it the Hall of Theogamy ("Marriage of the Gods"), while it's known as a Birth Chamber in standard Egyptology. Its purpose was to commemorate the divine birth of the king, and similar scenes can be found at the earlier Mortuary Temple of Hatshepsut on Luxor's west bank.

Later, throughout the Late Kingdom and Ptolemaic eras, pharaohs would regularly build Birth Chapels known as *mammisi* with similar artwork, albeit as standalone structures in a temple's outer court.

But what makes the scenes here at Luxor Temple special? One noteworthy detail is its anatomical correspondence. If you'll recall, the paving blocks of the covered portion of the temple form a mosaic of a pharaoh's face looking to the left. And when the face is examined together with the temple plan, this particular room corresponds to the vocal cords and thyroid gland, a gland which regulates growth.

While over in the Peristyle Court we saw the inscription referring to the physical birth of the king, the Hall of Theogamy is an homage to the pharaoh's spiritual birth. And when looking at the reliefs with the vocal cords in mind, one can't help but recall the opening of the Gospel of John: "In the beginning was the Word, and the Word was with God, and the Word was God."[4]

But long before the Bible was written, the Egyptians had a similar saying. One line from the Book of Coming Forth by Day (better known as the Book of the Dead) reads: "I am the Eternal, I am Ra. I am that which created the Word. I am the Word."[2] The Egyptians, therefore, were the first to declare that creation emerged out of vibration, or the "Word."

While the reliefs aren't in the best condition and the lighting is dim, it's still possible to follow an important set of scenes depicting Amenhotep III's divine birth. Located along the west wall, the

Fig. 58. The Hall of Theogamy

scenes are meant to be observed from bottom to top, with the bottom register moving from right to left and the next register moving from left to right.

Starting at the far right of the bottom register, we see Hathor embracing the pharaoh's mother, Mutmoia, who has been chosen to bear the divine pharaoh with the god Amun. We then see Amun himself receiving the news, who in turn sends Djehuty to proclaim (in this room that corresponds to the vocal cords) the special announcement.

Amun then takes the form of Tuthmosis IV, Amenhotep III's father. We then see Amun and Mutmoia, legs intertwined (fig. 59). According to the accompanying hieroglyphic inscription, "his dew filled her body." The pair is being lifted up by the goddesses Selkit, who represents an active, creative principle, and Neith, the goddess of weaving, who represents the invisible matrix.

The goddesses themselves appear to be floating on air, adding to the otherworldly and divine nature of the scene. Long before Christianity, this is one of the first mentions of an "Immaculate Conception."

The text continues, stating how Mutmoia "smelled his perfume" and "smiled to His Majesty." It further elaborates how Amun came to her "burning with desire," and how Mutmoia could see him "in his divine appearance." Amun's love then "took hold of her body, with the room being filled with the fragrance of the gods."

We see Amun holding the Ankh, a symbol of life, to the queen's nose, symbolizing the moment of conception.

To the left, we see Khnum, the ram-headed creator god, in the presence of Amun, who's likely instructing him to form the divine pharaoh. The Egyptians believed that Khnum formed all living things on his potter's wheel, and we next see him with what appears to be a small set of twins.

But it's really Amenhotep and his *ka*. As mentioned earlier, the Egyptians commonly depicted one's *ka* as their identical body double. We also see Hathor holding the Ankh up to the newly-formed child's nose, giving him life (fig. 60).

Fig. 59. The relief of Mutmoia's union with Amun in the Hall of Theogamy

Moving up to the next register (reading from left to right now), Djehuty announces to Mutmoia that she will indeed bear a son. We then see a pregnant Mutmoia taken to the delivery room by both Khnum and Hathor.

The child is then born, with the baby pharaoh being presented to the gods. It's a joyous occasion, and the gods offer their protection and promises of eternal life. The baby is then passed over to his true father, Amun, before being suckled by the great cow goddess, Hathor.

After being passed once more to Amun, the god's divine scribes, Djehuty and Seshat, write down the length of his reign.

As one might observe, in addition to the idea of the Immaculate Conception, numerous other aspects of these scenes, such as a visit by divine beings and the presence of a cow at birth, can be likened to the birth of Jesus described in the New Testament over a millennium later.

As Mutmoia was a commoner and succession to the throne was normally passed down matrilineally, some scholars claim that Amenhotep merely placed these reliefs in the temple to legitimize his reign. But if they were meant as propaganda for the general public, this was certainly the wrong place for it, as nobody but a small group of elite priests would've been allowed to see them!

Examining these scenes from the symbolist perspective, their purpose begins to make more sense. Luxor Temple is symbolic of man and his relationship with the cosmos. And the pharaoh in Egyptian society was a symbol of the Perfected Man. (Whether or not the pharaoh actually behaved in a perfect manner is irrelevant.)

From an esoteric point of view, matter is created by an unseen force which permeates through all creation. In this particular instance, the force is represented by Amun, who could be considered the divine father of all living things.

Caught up in the ups and downs of everyday life, we tend to forget this. That's why so many spiritual schools of thought, such as that of ancient Egypt along with Eastern philosophies such as

Advaita Vedanta, have emphasized the need to simply *remember* that we are all merely emanations of a single source.

Much like how Buddhists use images of the Buddha to meditate on one's inherent but hidden "Buddha nature," Egyptian priests likely used such scenes to contemplate on the divine within.

With all that being said, we also must consider the possibility that these scenes *were* perhaps intended as propaganda – not for the commoner, but for the priests themselves!

When imagining the hierarchical structure of Egyptian society, we tend to think of the royal family and the priesthood as a fairly cohesive unit at the top. While this may have been true in some eras of Egyptian history, this was far from the case during the reign of Amenhotep III. Throughout the 18th Dynasty, which saw the birth of the Egyptian Empire, the priesthood had been greatly enriched thanks to private donations from Amenhotep's predecessors.

With their power and influence growing, tensions with the royal family began to grow along with it. Therefore, in addition to their esoteric symbolism, it's possible that these scenes also served to remind the priests who was boss.

Another interesting aspect of the Hall of Theogamy is the pattern of its reliefs. While divine birth scenes are carved along the west wall, the south wall depicts purification rites that took place after the king's birth. Next, the east wall features coronation rituals, while the themes of celebration and victory (represented by the slaying of an oryx) are carved along the north wall.

As mentioned, the divine birth scenes form a zig-zag pattern, starting from left-to-right on the bottom register and right-to-left on the register above, and so on. Next, the south wall reliefs begin from right to left along the upper register, ultimately finishing at the bottom left. The reliefs on the other walls of the chamber follow a similar zig-zag pattern, ultimately wrapping around the entire room. If one follows the entire sequence of reliefs, the final scene appears on the lower left register of the north wall, just before the divine birth scenes begin.

Fig. 60. Hathor holding an Ankh up to a baby Amenhotep III and his ka

It's interesting how the cycle's final scene depicts an oryx being sacrificed. We previously discussed the symbolism of a similar scene in the Hypostyle Hall and how the oryx provided nourishment for the king's *ka*. Its placement here at the end of one cycle and just before the start of the divine birth sequence, then, is surely no coincidence.

Before leaving the Hall of Theogamy, the room which corresponds to the vocal cords, be sure to take a look above the doors leading to the outside. Here, the various royal names of the king are announced to the world.

There's also one more fascinating correspondence to contemplate in this room. It can't be a coincidence that when an image of an infant is superimposed over the closed portion of the temple (fig. 50), the Hall of Theogamy happens to align precisely with the baby's navel!

THE CENTRAL BARQUE SHRINE
(SHRINE OF ALEXANDER)

Nearly every Egyptian temple had a central sanctuary that served as home to the solar barque of the prominent deity worshipped there. Luxor Temple was no exception.

In most Egyptian temples, such shrines could be considered the structure's "Holy of Holies," the most sacred part of the temple and the room whose dimensions served as a "seed" for all other sections. Luxor Temple's case was a bit different, however, as the central room of the Triple Sanctuary further south should instead be considered the temple's "seed" and its true Holy of Holies. But more on that later.

Standing inside the Central Barque Shrine today, the barque itself, a symbol of the crescent moon that would typically transport small golden images of the gods, is missing. As a result, the chamber

Fig. 61. The Central Barque Shrine

Fig. 62. Alexander presenting offerings to Min-Amun

appears rather ordinary to the modern visitor. Like the other nearby chambers, the scenes here are largely ceremonial in nature, depicting the pharaoh presenting various offerings to Amun.

But there's more to this small chamber than first meets the eye. As you can learn more about on p91, Schwaller de Lubicz discovered two axes carved into the sub-floor of this chamber, one of which is known as the Axis of Amun. This axis connects the Central Barque Shrine with the Shrine of Hatshepsut in the Court of Ramesses II, and many of the reliefs are also similar, including two ram-headed djed pillars. The other axis discovered here is called the Longitudinal Axis, or the Axis of Khonsu. But as a result of recent restorations, both have been obscured by paving stones.

Interestingly, while originally constructed by Amenhotep III, the Central Barque Shrine was later dismantled and modified by Alexander the Great upon his conquest of Egypt. But Alexander, who either had great respect for Egyptian traditions or simply appropriated the culture as a means to propitiate his new subjects, kept many of the original reliefs intact.

As such, we can see both Amenhotep and Alexander, who lived a thousand years apart, depicted in the reliefs. They wear the crowns of Upper and Lower Egypt while performing the sacred rites for the ithyphallic Min-Amun (fig. 62).

Before Alexander's remodeling, the space was demarcated by four pillars, traces of which can still be seen on the floor surround- ing the shrine. At some point, the original altar for the barque was removed as well.

Fascinatingly, a small cavity was built into the wall of this ante-chamber that was just large enough for a man to fit inside. It was concealed by a removable stone, and some scholars suggest that this is where a priest would stand to act as the "voice" of Amun during religious ceremonies.

And that may very well be true, as this shrine corresponds to the mouth - at least when a front-facing skeleton is placed over the temple plan (fig. 3).

Thus far, we've covered a few different examples of reliefs with missing stones located in the room corresponding to that particular part of the body. And it's in the Shrine of Alexander that you'll find two reliefs in which a pharaoh's mouth is missing (fig. 63)! Both are located on the walls surround-ing the inner shrine, one being on the south wall to the right of the portal and the other on the east wall.

Fig. 63. A pharaoh with a missing mouth

THE TEMPLE AXES

During their years of taking measurements at Luxor Temple, Schwaller de Lubicz and his Luxor Group discovered that the ancient architects made use of three main axes when devising their temple plans.

Two of these axes were discovered chiseled into the sub-floor of the Central Barque Shrine, or Shrine of Alexander. For the sake of preserving them, Egyptian authorities covered up the axes with pebbles in the 1990s, after which they later concealed them with paving stones.

The builders of Luxor Temple also used a standard median axis which cuts certain sections of the temple in two equal parts.

But what did each axis signify and how were they used? According to Schwaller, each axis was based on a particular theme or principle.

The different axes also help give the temple something akin to a subtle pivoting motion. In other words, in this temple consecrated to development and growth, the axes help the structure escape the rigidity imposed by matter.

Furthermore, the splitting of the three axes may also represent the splitting of Unity to multiplicity. And as we'll cover below, the geometric relationship between the various axes was also of major significance.

The three main axes are as follows:

The Median Axis / The Axis of Mut (33° 00' east of north):

This axis divides the original covered portion of the temple (from the Triple Sanctuary to the Hypostyle Hall) into two equal parts. While marked beneath the platform of the central room of the Triple Sanctuary, its "influence works in an occult manner," according to Schwaller.[1]

When looking at the temple map, you'll see certain sections of the temple gradually shifting to the east, with a dramatic shift taking place at the Court of Ramesses II. Accordingly, what Schwaller calls the Axis of Mut had to shift multiple times with each new construction phase. But this was far from being the result of sloppiness.

As mentioned, the Axis of Mut perfectly bisects the covered portion of the temple. It then deviates 3° in order to divide the both Peristyle Court and the Colonnade (the final portions built by Amenhotep III) into two equal parts.

Interestingly, the Median Axis here forms an angle of 36° relative to the north-south axis. This angle is important in the formation of a pentagon, which Schwaller calls the "soul of all vital movement."[5]

At the Court of Ramesses II, the axis deviates again by 7° 27'. If you'll recall, that portion of the temple represents man taking a forward step.

Reaching the pylon, the axis deviates slightly once again. This new line stretches all the way across the Avenue of the Sphinxes until it reaches Karnak. This final deviation forms a 45° angle relative to the north-south axis.

According to Schwaller, the Axis of Mut corresponds to the element of fire. He also refers to it as the Geometric and the Astronomical Axis.

The Longitudinal Axis / The Axis of Khonsu (33° 34' east of north):

This is one of the axes that was traced under the paving stones of the Central Barque Shrine. It then intersects with the Axis of Amun in the Offering Vestibule (fig. 66).

Fig. 64. The Axis of Amun from the Central
Barque Shrine to the Shrine of Hatshepsut

Fig. 65. The Axis of Mut and its shifts
throughout the temple

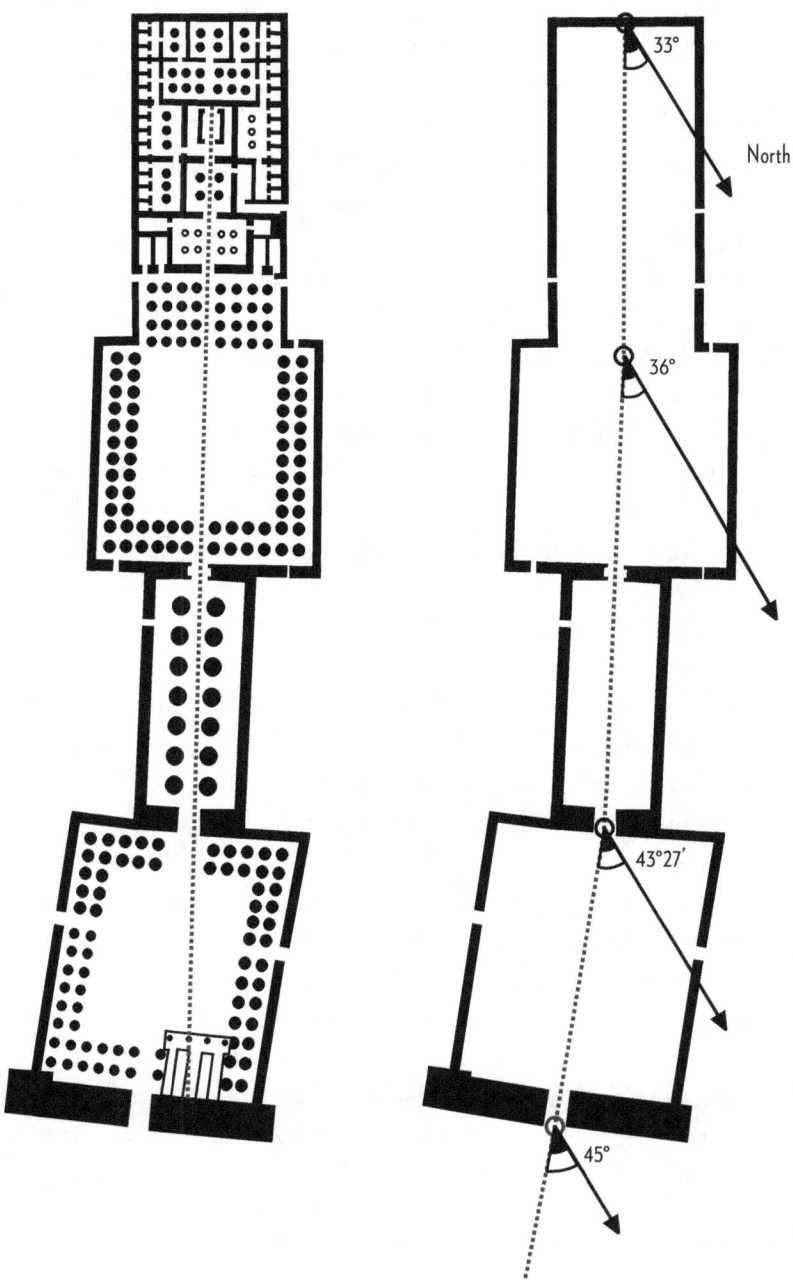

This axis divides the southern, or the original covered portion of the temple into two unequal parts, which Schwaller believed to be connected with solar influence. For example, the sun at its zenith in midday does not precisely divide the day into two equal halves.

Furthermore, the strength of the sun's rays, not to mention the quality of the sun's radiation, are not the same at different points in the day. But such variation is necessary for things on earth to grow in the manner in which they do.

Schwaller, therefore, believed that such a variation was vital to bring the temple to "life." While not visible to the casual observer, certain temple walls were built parallel to this axis, deliberately giving the temple layout an uneven yet organic feel.

The Longitudinal Axis, which is closely related to themes such as movement and growth, could also be called the Solar Axis and the General Axis of Measures.

The Axis of Amun (34° 27' east of north):

This axis was also found hammered into the floor of the Central Barque Shrine. What's especially remarkable is that it directly connects the barque shrine with the Shrine of Hatshepsut, or the way station found in the Court of Ramesses II.

The starting point of the axis was marked in the Central Barque Shrine by two ram-headed *djed* pillars, symbols which both represented the backbone of Osiris and the stability of the universe. Incredibly, the exact point where the Axis of Amun ends in the Shrine of Hatshepsut is also marked by two ram-headed *djed* pillars!

Schwaller de Lubicz discovered that the Axis of Amun essentially bisects the entire temple, forming a long rectangle that's "determined to the millimeter by the hypotenuse of a 1:7 triangle," writes John Anthony West.[2]

It's clear then, that the Axis of Amun and the relative positions of these two shrines played a major role in the planning of the entire temple (see p112).

According to Schwaller, this axis also represents the principles of sex, procreation and water. In particular, he believed the axis was intended to infuse the temple with the generative power of Min-Amun.

GOING DEEPER

You may still be wondering how the temple builders came up with these particular axes. That's where things start to get a lot more complex.

In *The Temple of Man*, Schwaller de Lubicz goes on to explain exactly how and why Luxor Temple's designers chose these particular angles and not any others. He provides the reader with numerous diagrams and complex mathematical formulas which demonstrate how these axes functioned in particular parts of the temple.

Additionally, the different angles formed by the axes in relation to the north-south axis, as well as to each other, all had particular functions and meanings - both geometrically and ideologically.

Such research cannot merely be summarized and must be carefully studied to be fully understood. Schwaller points out, however, that the various angles formed by the axes hint at the interplay between the hexagon and the pentagon, two shapes that play a vital role in creation.

The three architectural axes of the temple of Luxor are, for the mystic Temple, the vital function represented by Amun-Mut and their fruit, Khonsu.[5]

The Axis of Khonsu
(Longitudinal Axis)　　　The Axis of Amun

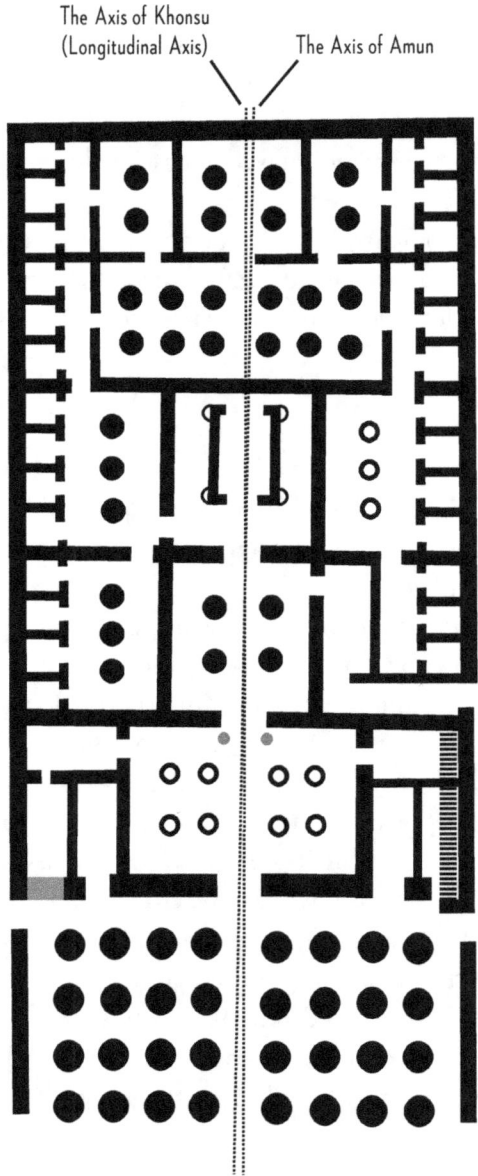

Fig. 66. The intersection of the Axes of Amun and Khonsu in the covered temple

THE TEMPLE WITHIN THE TEMPLE

As you make your way south from the Central Barque Shrine, bear in mind that the next doorway was never part of the original temple plan. For initiates walking straight through Luxor Temple from the pylon entrance, it's here that they would've hit a dead-end.

Beyond the wall was an even more sacred portion of the temple referred to as *ipt ryst*, or the "Southern Opet." The original entrance to this "temple within a temple" would've been via a portal to the west.

Schwaller de Lubicz spends a significant portion of his book *The Temple in Man* pointing out the myriad of similarities between the layouts of European Gothic cathedrals and that of Luxor Temple. It's entirely possible that the builders of these cathedrals based their blueprints on principles that originated in Egypt and were secretly passed down over the centuries. With that in mind, a close examination of the different functions of a medieval Gothic cathedral could perhaps reveal more about how Luxor Temple operated.

At special cathedrals that were qualified to host the papal mass, the bishop's throne would be hidden from the public behind the altar, and it's there that he would celebrate the Sacrament in private. Similarly, we should think of the rooms beyond the Central Barque Shrine as a private section of the temple where the most sacred of rites would be carried out by the head priest.

Today, we can take advantage of the modern passageway that leads to the next hall, so let's continue heading directly south.

THE HALL OF TWELVE COLUMNS

········ ☥ ········

Past the Central Barque Shrine is the Hall of Twelve Columns, known as the "Hall of the Offering Tablet" in Dynastic times. It's flanked by two smaller rooms on either side, with the eastern one going by the same name (*wsekhet hetep*) in ancient Egyptian.

This part of the temple corresponds to the eyes when a front-facing skeleton is superimposed over the temple plan. Those familiar with Egyptian symbolism will be aware of the "Eye of Ra," which itself is a symbol of the sun.

The Egyptians did not believe that Ra was actually the sun, but rather, "The sun was the eye of [Ra]; in other words, the perceiving organ of divinity and the physical manifestation of the invisible cause."[3]

Fig. 67. The Hall of Twelve Columns

Interestingly, the Hall of Twelve Columns, which Schwaller labels as "room 12," contains symbolism related to both the optical nerve center of the human body and the trajectory of the sun.

As we know, both the day and night are comprised of twelve hours (the chamber, in fact, is also commonly referred to as the "Hall of Hours"). But what's more, is that there are precisely twelve optical nerves at the point where two brain hemispheres unite.

"The medulla oblongata, from which stem the twelve pairs of cranial nerves, ends in the west side of room 12," writes Schwaller de Lubicz. "From the medulla the marrow continues into the spinal column, and from the marrow stem all the sensory and motor spinal nerves."[1]

As we discussed earlier, both this room and the west pylon in the front of the temple are twelve fathoms long, emphasizing the link between this part of the brain and the feet via the central nervous channel. Just as how everything in our body is connected in one way or another, the same can be said about Luxor Temple and the myriad of symbolical relationships between its different parts.

Further symbolism in room 12 relates to the polarity between east and west. In ancient Egypt, east, the direction of the rising sun, was associated with concepts like birth, potential and resurrection. The west, in contrast, represented death and the concept of completion.

The temple builders left behind numerous clues to emphasize this polarity, though some of them are extremely subtle. One example is that of the vultures, a symbol of the goddess Nekhbet, who in turn represented the concept of assimilation.

Originally depicted on both the eastern and western sides of the middle portal of the southern wall, the eastern vulture has unfortunately completely vanished. But if still visible, visitors could observe how the eastern vulture was depicted as partially unfinished, while the western relief is complete.

Fig. 68. Sacrificial bulls

The east-west dichotomy is further emphasized by the reliefs of the sacrificial bulls. On the northern wall, the trussed bulls on the eastern side are facing the hall's interior (fig. 68). They have yet to be slaughtered and represent the concept of potential. Those on the west, meanwhile, have already been killed and their backs are facing the room. Their life cycle has come to an end.

Yet another distinction between east and west cannot even be seen by the naked eye but through the sense of touch. While each set of six columns appears identical, be sure to run your hands over the flutings (fig. 69). On the eastern side, the flutings of the columns are semicircular and smooth, representing Unity. The flutings of the western columns, in contrast, are ogival - a result of the connection between two points. Hence, the flutings here represent Duality.

Fig. 69. The flutings of the columns

Despite the subtlety, it's not difficult to feel the difference. It adds further weight to the argument that the Egyptians saw their temples not merely as places of worship, but as three-dimensional books.

In addition to the optical system, this room also corresponds to the olfactory system, which regulates the sense of smell. As seen throughout the temple, certain areas simultaneously feature correspondences to both a front-facing and profile view of a human skeleton. And the Hall of Twelve Columns, or room 12, is no different.

For this next subtle but amazing correspondence, let's once again recall the mosaic face looking off to the side that was formed by the paving blocks throughout the covered portion of the temple (fig. 49). As we'll go over shortly, the next section of the temple to the south is the Triple Sanctuary, and the easternmost room there – which Schwaller calls room 5 – shares a wall with room 12. The reliefs on either side of this wall demonstrate what Schwaller refers to as "transposition."

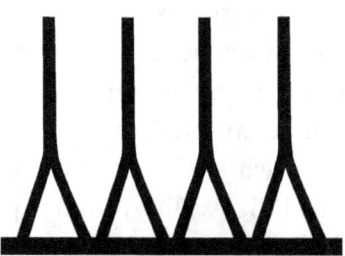

Fig. 70. The hieroglyph for fabrics

At numerous Egyptian temples, reliefs on one side of a wall would sometimes have a direct relationship with the reliefs on its opposite side, almost as if the stone were transparent. Only by taking both sides into account could the initiate get the full picture.

In this case, the wall in room 12 contains the symbol for fabrics. The hieroglyph for fabrics happens to closely represent the olfactory bulb, which regulates our sense of smell (fig. 70). In fact, when the side view of a human head is placed over this portion of the temple, the wall between rooms 12 and 5 lines up perfectly with the location of the olfactory bulb!

But what's on the other side of the wall? In room 5, we can see glyphs for "boxes for cloths," or the *mrt* boxes discussed earlier (fig. 51). It would appear, then, that the fabrics on one side are intended for the boxes on the other.

The temple builders were surely hinting at the link between different nerves and tracts within the human head, and they clearly knew exactly where these connections were made. According to John Anthony West, "the action of warp and weft is the Egyptian way of symbolising the 'crossing' that is characteristic of the mental process."[2]

In regards to reliefs which contain missing stones mentioned in previous sections, this single hall contains several additional examples, according to Schwaller. Confusingly, however, the examples in this room appear slightly different from the illustrations he provides in *The Temple of Man*.

For example, in some instances, the stones aren't missing but appear to have been put back in place. And in other cases, the reliefs are too badly damaged to tell which stones may have been missing since ancient times.

Nevertheless, on the south wall, close to the center, we see two different reliefs of Amenhotep III where a cut has been made in the stone near his eyes. And over on the eastern wall is a similar example involving a goddess. On the western wall, meanwhile, in the area which corresponds to the back of the head, Schwaller found a pharaoh herding cattle with that part of his head missing!

Again, the supposed "missing stones" are especially hard to spot in this hall, with not all of them even missing. We don't know how this room appeared a century ago during Schwaller's stay in Luxor, though there do seem to be enough anomalies in the masonry to suggest that the builders left behind deliberate clues.

Taking a brief break from all the symbolism, look up above the walls to see if you can find where the influential surrealist poet Arthur Rimbaud once carved his name.

Your memory and your senses are but the nourishment of your creative impulse. - Arthur Rimbaud[6]

THE TRIPLE SANCTUARY

········ ☥ ········

Last, but certainly not least, at the far southern edge of the temple, is what's known as the Triple Sanctuary. As mentioned earlier, only the very highest-ranked initiates would be allowed inside here, and this was likely the very first portion of the temple built (at least during Amenhotep III's reign). It could also be considered Luxor Temple's true Holy of Holies.

Luxor Temple's original name of *ipt rsyt* (Southern Sanctuary) was named after this section, and it was constructed over a low mound that was believed to be the original site of creation (though, to be fair, there are many such places throughout Egypt!).

Its center consists of a small room with four columns, with even smaller rooms containing two columns each on either side. Originally roofed over, the sanctuary is now open to the elements,

Fig. 71. The Triple Sanctuary's central chamber

Fig. 72. The eastern room of the Triple Sanctuary (room 5)

and the best vantage point is actually from the street just beyond the temple complex.

From outside the eastern walls, you'll notice some seemingly random decorations. Some scholars believe that the wall was used for practice by the artisans who'd go on to decorate the rest of the temple. Another possibility is that some of these stones were usurped from an even older incarnation of the temple built during the Middle Kingdom period.

With that in mind, the apparent randomness of these stones may have had symbolic intent. Upside-down images, for example, were possibly used to act as "seeds" out of which new constructions were meant to grow.

Still on the outside, but along the exterior wall of the central chamber, notice the Ankh symbol in the middle of the wall (fig. 74). It likely demarcates the origin of the Axis of Mut, or the Median Axis which splits the entire covered temple in two perfect halves. This axis will later intersect with the

Axis of Amun to symbolically "give birth" to the Axis of Khonsu (see p91).

Stepping inside, the central room of the Triple Sanctuary was once the location of a colossal seated statue of Amun (fig. 71). While the statue is gone, part of its base can still be seen. In particular, the form of Amun worshipped here was known as Amenemope (not to be confused with numerous princes of the same name).

Amenemope, which means Amun of Opet, was a form of the local fertility god, and it represented the aspect of Amun specifically worshipped at Luxor. Nearby Karnak, in contrast, was consecrated to Amun-Ra.

Anatomically speaking, it is the central room which corresponds to the pineal gland, dubbed by mystics as the "Third Eye." Many world cultures, especially those of the East, have claimed that it's this mysterious pea-shaped gland that's responsible for mystical visions and contact with higher realms.

In ancient Egypt, the location of the pineal gland was marked by the Uraeus, a symbol depicting a cobra emanating from the forehead of the pharaoh, indicating the state of being in constant communion with the gods.

The two smaller rooms, according to Schwaller de Lubicz, represent the pituitary gland, of which there are two parts: anterior and posterior. Together, they produce hormones that regulate important functions like growth, metabolism, reproduction and blood pressure.

Furthermore, the Triple Sanctuary also marks the location of the hypothalamus, the part of the brain which helps keep the body in a constant state of homeostasis.

From a symbolist perspective, this section of the temple not only represents the generative principles of creation, but man's direct link with a state of higher consciousness. But let's take an even deeper look by examining the meaning behind the Triple Sanctuary's emphasis on *three*.

Fig. 73. The Triple Sanctuary as seen from the south

Fig. 74. The Ankh marking the start of the Axis of Mut

In accordance with universal law, a perfect manifestation cannot be produced without the union of two opposing forces. A child can only be born from male and female parents, while positive and negative charges are required to produce electricity.

When two complementary forces harmonize, what results is a third force that's distinct from the first two yet which contains qualities of each. Adept initiates will recognize this as the "law of the triangle."

Accordingly, the Egyptians commonly worshipped deities in triads. In addition to the Theban Triad mentioned earlier, they also revered the Memphite Triad of Ptah-Skehmet-Nefertum and the Osirian Triad, whose mythology adorns countless tomb and temple walls.

In the Hermetic tradition, Hermes Trismegistus (Hermes Three Times Great) became a Perfected Man by overcoming the three worlds: the spiritual world of the imagination, the mental world of personality and the physical world of gross matter. And in Plato's *Republic*, he talks about the tripartite nature of the soul (rational, spirited and appetitive). These esoteric concepts could surely be traced back to the initiatory lineages of ancient Egypt.

Rather than stay trapped in rational, dualistic thinking, a true seeker must reconcile and transcend opposing forces through the "Intelligence of the Heart." Only then can one's spiritual goals be realized.

Architecturally, the central chamber of the Triple Sanctuary was likely the seed on which the rest of the temple was based. A relief on its western wall gives us a clue, as here we can see five reliefs of the pharaoh in the presence of both Amun and Min-Amun.

While each king is of the same height, their heads gradually change in size. As the size of a human's head in relation to its body can reveal a person's age, Schwaller de Lubicz considered this series of images to represent the pharaoh's growth and development.

The reliefs, however, don't merely depict the growth of the king. Their dimensions and proportions also reveal secret information about the planned growth of Luxor Temple itself, among other things.

John Anthony West elaborates:

> Measuring these kings, Schwaller de Lubicz found them gradually increasing in size. Each king measures exactly seventy-two digits, the digits being fractions of the different values of cubit, each of which is founded upon exact geodesic considerations: the difference between them is determined by the degree of latitude to which the measure pertains.

Schwaller de Lubicz then shows how the relationships between these different measures are connected to the notes of the musical scale, to the axes of the Temple and to the fundamental grid based upon nineteen squares. [2]

Speaking of the musical scale, while this chamber appears at first glance to be perfectly square, it isn't. The proportions of the chamber are in the ratio of 8:9, or that of the first musical note of an octave. And the part of the brain (the hypothalamus and pituitary center) which this chamber represents could be likened to a musical composer, creating harmony and homeostasis within our entire system.

On a spiritual level, this part of the brain is our psychic center, responsible for composing the "notes" which help us resonate harmonically with otherwise unseen realities. And in regards to the temple plan, it was this chamber that struck the first note, so to speak, with its proportions serving as the basis for all subsequent parts. What resulted is the complex symphony we now know as Luxor Temple.

As mentioned, the Triple Sanctuary marks the southern extremity of the temple. But if you overlay a skeleton over the temple plan, something is missing: the skull's cranium. But why?

THE MISSING CROWN

If all the correspondences between the temple plan and the human body mentioned thus far are correct, one wonders why the builders didn't even leave a little bit of room for the crown. This omission is especially puzzling for those familiar with Hindu philosophy, in which the top of the crown is the seat of the highest of the chakras, or the energy center closest to the divine source.

According to Schwaller de Lubicz, however, the crown's absence at Luxor Temple was entirely deliberate. For it's also this part of the brain that's responsible for making distinctions and for controlling the ego.

Amazingly, even modern scientific discoveries back this up. The cranium is known to contain a dense amount of von Economo Neurons (VENs), named after the German scientist Constantin von Economo. Though they were discovered during Schwaller's lifetime in the 1920s, it's only recently that scientists have found a link between these neurons and our sense of "I."

Obviously, we need this part of the brain to normally function in the world. But Luxor Temple doesn't represent an ordinary state of consciousness. It represents the Perfected Man, or man before the acquisition of ego. And the spiritual goal of every human is to return to this state of egolessness and perfection.

Advanced yogis have been known to suppress VENs through rigorous meditation practice. And upon doing so, they can enter a state of consciousness known as Samadhi, a trance-like state in which an individual achieves union with the divine while still in the human body.

While we can't be certain of exactly what spiritual disciplines were practiced by ancient Egyptian initiates, it's clear that they were intuitively aware of VENs in the cranium. Like the Indian yogis, they likely also knew of methods to suppress VENs (or, in less scientific terms, the "monkey mind") in order to experience mystical visions.

An intimate knowledge of these subjects is demonstrated by the royal diadem worn by

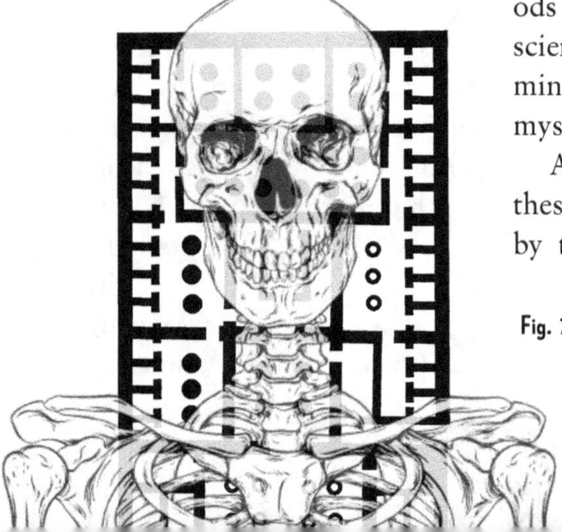

Fig. 75. The hypothetical skeleton's cranium above the temple layout

Egyptian pharaohs, particularly that of Tutankhamun. Emanating from the forehead (or Third Eye) is a combination of a cobra and vulture, representing the unification of Upper and Lower Egypt.

Symbolically, the cobra also represents the intellect and the brain's capacity to discriminate, while the vulture represents synthesis and assimilation. The cobra's body also forms an arch over the cranium, precisely where the brain's hemispheres divide.

Such concepts are even emphasized in two-dimensional art. Nearly all Egyptian art was based on a precise grid system of eighteen squares. The artists calculated a figure's proportions based on the location of its forehead - not the top of the skull. The eighteenth square was then divided by the Golden Section, or phi, to determine the location of the navel, which fell around the eleventh square.

Of course, an additional 19th square (or more) was utilized to depict the individual's cranium or headgear. But it's the forehead and its relationship with phi that determined the overall proportions. And it's this same method, Schwaller believed, that was used to calculate the harmonic proportions of Luxor Temple, the Temple of Man. "From averages established from measurements of the human body, it has been proved that the navel divides the total height of the body in the proportion of phi to 1," he writes.[1]

Like many aspects of ancient Egyptian art, this concept later found its way into Christian symbolism. A 14th-century statue of the 5th-century martyr St. Nicasius of Rheims, for example, depicts the

Fig. 76. Amenhotep III and his Uraeus

saint carrying the cranium of

his own head - a symbol of mastery over one's ego. As we've discussed, this emphasis on self-mastery can be found repeatedly throughout the temple and its surroundings, from the open-air Avenue of the Sphinxes to the secluded and mysterious Holy of Holies.

CONCLUSION

The correspondences discovered by Schwaller de Lubicz range from the strikingly clear (such as the striding colossi symbolizing the lower leg and the inscription at the spot of the navel) to the extemely subtle (the moon's relation to the lungs and the unfinished eastern reliefs in the Hall of Twelve Columns).

In addition to the basic concepts, this book also brings forth some of the more obscure or often overlooked aspects of Schwaller's symbolist approach. But it merely scratches the surface of all the connections between the temple architecture, the human form and cosmic laws. Schwaller de Lubicz's monumental opus *The Temple of Man*, in fact, spans over 1,000 pages!

Based on what we've gone over thus far, however, it's undeniable that the ancient Egyptians operated at a much higher level of sophistication than Egyptologists commonly give them credit for. And while thousands of years may have passed, the messages encoded in their massive stone monuments can still teach us important lessons today.

To fully grasp the symbolist perspective of Luxor Temple, one must study it in detail and, better yet, experience it firsthand. But the temple and its teaching can also be summed up in a single sentence: "Know Thyself."

The Temple of Luxor is itself an initiatic text, an expression of a total understanding of the creation of Adamic man. It embodies the teaching and it is the teaching." - John Anthony West[2]

LUXOR TEMPLE'S HIDDEN ORIGINS

Amenhotep, son of Hapu was indisputably one of ancient Egypt's greatest-ever architects. But when closely scrutinizing Luxor Temple's history, one begins to wonder if the temple plans entirely date from his time.

As previously discussed, the earliest constructions in the area of Luxor Temple were built during the Middle Kingdom. And some Middle Kingdom stones were likely reused in various existing structures.

Following Hyksos rule, construction resumed in the area during the 18th Dynasty – albeit two centuries before the reign of Amenhotep III! An inscription found at a quarry east of Memphis states that the dynasty's first pharaoh, Ahmose I (r. 1549–1524 BC) had limestone cut for construction at Luxor Temple, then known as the "Southern Sanctuary."

Later on in the 18th Dynasty, but still before Amenhotep III's reign, we also know that six way stations were built along the Avenue of the Sphinxes during the joint reign of Hatshepsut and Thutmosis III. This is evidenced by relief carvings of the Opet Festival uncovered at Karnak.

And in the Court of Ramesses II, the Shrine of Hatshepsut likely served as the sixth and final way station. It was here that the sacred barques of Amun (and later Mut and Khonsu) were ritually cleansed as part of the procession.

Egyptologists, however, are still divided on this structure's true origins. Has it largely been left in place since the time of Hatshepsut and Thutmosis III, with Ramesses II using its orientation as a reference for his new court? Or did Ramesses II build an entirely new structure?

Looking closely, the shrine contains numerous clues which tell us it was indeed constructed during Hatshepsut's reign.

Fig. 77. The Shrine of Hatshepsut's central chamber

One example can be found on the upper architrave outside the main structure. The carving of a duck (or perhaps a goose) has two feathers – exactly how they were typically drawn during the 18th Dynasty. By the 19th Dynasty, in contrast, they would be depicted with three.

Another clue is revealed by the hieroglyphs on the columns. Like many languages today, the ancient Egyptian language used both masculine and feminine forms of various words. Hatshepsut, of course, was a rare female pharaoh. And during her reign, the common phrase "beloved of Amun" was feminized by adding the glyph for T at the end.

So while Hatshepsut's royal cartouches were later recarved with those of Ramesses II, the artisans forgot to remove the feminized form of the remaining phrases!

We can surmise, then, that most of the extant pieces of the shrine were carved and assembled during Hatshepsut's reign. What's still not totally clear, however, is whether or not the shrine's current orientation is original or if it was later repositioned by Ramesses II.

But why is this so important? It's because if the structure is still in the same position it was already in during Amenhotep III's reign, then Amenhotep, son of Hapu would've based his entire design plan with the Shrine of Hatshepsut's exact position in mind.

As we discussed, even with the skewed position of the Ramesses court, the Axis of Amun directly connects the way station's back wall with the Central Barque Shrine, one of the most sacred parts of the temple. Additionally, the relief carvings in both structures appear to be mirror images of one another, with the starting and ending points of the axis marked in both shrines by ram-headed *djed* pillars.

Clearly, the relative positions of the Shrine of Hatshepsut and the Central Barque Shrine dictate the rest of Luxor Temple's geometry, proportions and overall balance.

As was common in Egypt, the dimensions of the oldest part of a temple would often be used to determine the measurements of the rest of the temple - much like a seed. But if the Shrine of Hatshepsut is indeed right where Hatshepsut left it, we could think of it as the "seed of the seed." And if that's the case, it would also be reasonable to assume that the general temple plan predates Amenhotep III's reign!

Things get even more interesting when we look at the teachings of the Rosicrucians. According to Rosicrucian sacred history, Tuthmosis III established the first esoteric school of initiates, organizing various Egyptian mystical sects into a single unified order.

Most Egyptologists suspect that the relationship between Thutmosis III and Hatshepsut was icy at best, if not outright hostile. This is because Thutmosis, the rightful heir to the throne, was too young to rule at the time of his father's death, prompting Hatshepsut to declare herself pharaoh. The Rosicrucians, on the other hand, have a different take.

They believe that Hatshepsut and Thutmosis III cooperated to establish a new mystery school at Karnak along with Hatshepsut's most trusted vizier, chief and high priest, Hapuseneb. Could Amenhotep, son of Hapu have been later initiated into this same order?

We also mustn't forget Hatshepsut's head architect, Senemut, who constructed the masterpiece we now call the Mortuary Temple of Hatshepsut in Deir el Bahari. This temple, however, was obviously based on the design of the earlier Middle Kingdom temple right next to it. And it was the Middle Kingdom pharaohs who initiated constructions at both Karnak and the area around Luxor Temple.

Though we lack any conclusive evidence, it's entirely possible that the original idea for Luxor Temple not only predates Amenhotep III's reign, but also the entire New Kingdom period!

Whether or not Amenhotep, son of Hapu devised the temple plan himself, he certainly deserves credit for being the one to finally carry it out. But in a broader sense, Luxor Temple, the Temple of Man, shouldn't be thought of as an accomplishment of one single individual. Rather, it's the fruit of wisdom maintained and passed down in Egypt through countless generations – wisdom that we can still study and learn from today.

PRACTICAL APPLICATIONS

As previously discussed, Luxor Temple could be likened to a three-dimensional book. But having "read" Luxor Temple, many visitors will find themselves wondering how to begin using the knowledge and wisdom in a practical way.

We can only speculate on the exact rituals, meditations and mantras used by the Egyptian priesthood and pharaohs in ancient times. We can, however, look to mystery schools such as the Rosicrucians, who claim a direct, unbroken lineage to the ancient priesthood of Egypt.

In addition to Rosicrucian techniques, the following Practical Applications are a synthesis of various esoteric and mystical traditions that are rooted in universal principles. All of the following exercises are intended to help you achieve self-transformation as you make your way through the Temple of Man.

LOCATION: AVENUE OF THE SPHINXES
EXERCISE: MENTAL STILLNESS

THE MANTRA

Our first practical application was created by John Anthony West (see p8), and is something he would have all of his tour groups do during their visits to Luxor Temple.

After purchasing your ticket, avert your eyes from the temple and walk away from it with your back to the temple facade. Walk slowly, ceremonially and quietly up the Avenue of the Sphinxes to a comfortable distance, about twenty sphinxes in. Then proceed to turn around and look at the temple facade. (If you're visiting Luxor Temple via the long walk along the Avenue of the Sphinxes from Karnak, you can begin this exercise as soon as Luxor Temple comes into view in the distance.)

Bring your attention within. Shift your awareness into your feet. With each step, keep your focus on your feet, repeating aloud the phrase "I am here, I am here, I am here."

In the Eastern alchemical tradition, the looping of a single phrase or word is called a mantra.

Give yourself space after every "I am here" to try to determine what this really means. You will find that giving this utterance conscious consideration transforms the phrase from mere words into a living thought.

As time goes on, distinctions between the observer and the observed, or in other words, between you and your consciousness, will gradually begin to fade.

LOCATION: THE FORECOURT OF NECTANEBO
EXERCISE: MENTAL STILLNESS

THE ROSICRUCIAN / RAMESSES TECHNIQUE

Proceed toward the southwest area of the forecourt. Choose to sit on either the bench or steps in front of the west pylon.

Keep your posture with your back as straight as possible, with your feet touching the floor and the palms of your hands on your knees.

Keep your elbows square, the preferred meditation position of the Rosicrucians. As you'll notice, this is the same position of the colossal seated Ramesses statues at the temple entrance.

A point to keep in mind is that as mentioned earlier, the sacred history of the Rosicrucian Order traces its tradition back to ancient Egypt.

Sit in stillness. Observe silence (if possible, visit the temple early in the morning). You may close your eyes or keep gazing outwardly with your physical eyes, but direct your consciousness inward. Pay attention to the rhythm of your breath.

Remain in a state of meditation for several moments, or however long you feel comfortable. With that being said, pushing yourself to practice mental stillness longer than normal will gradually help you achieve self-mastery and discipline.

This meditation exercise in the forecourt will help prepare you for later exercises.

Why are you so enchanted with this world
when a mine of gold lies within you?
Open your eyes and come -
Return to the root of the root
of your own soul - Rumi[7]

LOCATION: THE PYLON & PORTAL (THE FEET)
EXERCISE: INNER FOCUS

THE BATTLE OF KADESH MASTERY MEDITATION

When looking at the pylon, we are confronted with the Battle of Kadesh. This battle brings to mind the four stages of a focused mind as expressed in the Zen and Daoist traditions of the Far East. The four stages are as follows:

1. One Mind
2. Clear Mind
3. Immovable Mind
4. Complete Mind

In the more cerebral material arts traditions, the journey from emptiness through fullness and back to emptiness is the journey to mastery. - Stratton Horres & Michala Perreault[8]

Like seeming opposites of day and night or light and darkness, the Battle of Kadesh represents the blending and merging of polarized energies.

Following the swirling path from one energy through the other and back again is how you achieve balance. It is when the energies are in balance that you go right into stillness. Spending all your time in one energy with little or no influence from the other leaves you out of balance: you never complete the circle, and the path to mastery takes much longer.[8]

It is through the union of force and flow that we create a "meditative state," enabling us to get into the "zone."

1. One Mind means focusing your attention on a single purpose or goal, much like the Hermetic expression "all is mind."

It's hard to get any one thing done when your mind is trying to keep track of numerous tasks or bits of information simultaneously.

How was Ramesses able to lay waste to scores of enemies? By taking on one at a time.

Give one single thing your full attention so that you may accomplish it thoroughly. As for what that one single thing should be, the choice is yours.

As discussed throughout the main portion of the book, the purpose of Luxor Temple and the Egyptian philosophy as a whole was to establish a deep connection with the divine and ultimately a return to the source. But this is obviously no easy task. In fact, it's the most difficult goal of them all.

Therefore, for now, you may want to decide to focus your attention on something more obtainable in the near future. Later on, after experiencing the amazing things you can accomplish with deep inner focus, you can then set your sights on the ultimate goal - achieving the state that the Rosicrucians call "Peace Profound."

2. Clear Mind means having a quiet or empty mind, or what some refer to as "the void." This can be likened to the concept of "quieting the monkey mind" in Eastern traditions.

When you go into a state of clear mind like Ramesses on the battlefield, you can tap into Amun, the hidden universal force that permeates all life, allowing that power to work through you.

You are operating from a state of divine grace. If you'll recall, Ramesses was cut off from his troops, which could be seen as a metaphor for detaching oneself from external stimuli.

A true master can vanquish all enemies in what might seem like a hopeless battle when operating from an empty space. This state allows us to remain calm, open and ready for any unexpected event, able to move in concert with the universal force.

3. Immovable Mind means having an unwavering or unstoppable mind. As mentioned in step one, you must first identify a single target. You then must master the art of intensely focusing on your goal without any distractions. Then nothing will be able to stop you.

A famous scene from the Indian epic *The Mahabharata* involves a conversation between the teacher Drona and his archery students. Having placed a target, a wooden bird, in a tree, he challenged his disciples to bring it down with a single arrow.

But before even giving them a chance to shoot, he asked each one what they could see. Those who mentioned the tree, the branch or even the feathers of the bird were told to step down. The master knew they wouldn't strike their target with a single shot, and it was better that they not waste their arrows.

Last, however, came the top pupil, Arjuna, whose focus was so intent that he couldn't describe anything but the bird's head.

4. Complete Mind, as the name suggests, is defined by a state of completion. It is the state of mind that carries you through to an end. At the end of the story mentioned above, Drona gave Arjuna permission to shoot, and he did indeed bring down the bird on his first attempt.

Standing before the east pylon, imagine yourself as one of the nine archers (see p27), focusing so intently that you fire your arrow not just at the target, but all the way through it.

Next, it's time to come full circle. After Complete Mind, return to Clear Mind in order to prepare for what's to come next.

> In the mystical sense, the archer who still dualizes by sighting the target and has not himself become the arrow, does not attain unity, is not yet conscious, but remains only mortally and mentally aware.[5]

THE BATTLE WITHIN

Only after vanquishing the enemy, one may enter the temple. The Battle of Kadesh, when understood esoterically, emulates the battle of light over the forces of darkness. This battle in the Egyptian tradition is also represented by the contentions between Horus and Set.

Horus represents the principle of return to the source while Set represents both our animal nature and anything that comes in the way of us achieving full realization.

In the Christian tradition, of course, the conflict is represented by Christ and Satan. But in contrast to the later Christians, the Egyptians revered Set for the simple fact that the principle of opposition is necessary for the perpetuation of this world.

Furthermore, without opposition, there can be no path to self-mastery in the first place. Thus, despite believing Set to be a dark force, the Egyptians were aware of the futility of eliminating Set and his minions entirely. While he could indeed be defeated, he'd inevitably regenerate again and again until the final goal – a return to the source – could be achieved.

In regards to the principle of opposition, the teachings of the great mystic G.I. Gurdjieff tell us of the Yezidis, who believe that both good and evil exist in the mind and spirit of all humans.

Melek Taus, one of the seven angels of the Yezidis, is a representation of the principle of opposition, though not in quite the same way as Set. In Yezidi mythology, Melek Taus, also known as the peacock angel, is commanded by God to bow before Adam, the first man.

But Melek Taus refused, for he only wanted to bow directly to God and not one of his creations. Despite his disobedience, Melek Taus was rewarded, for it had all been a test. The Yezidis now worship Melek Taus as God's main representative on earth.

Nevertheless, outsiders have long accused the Yezidis of "devil worship" for their reverence of the one who dared defy God's orders. For those who understand the wisdom of the myth, however, Melek Taus reminds us that opposition is not always a bad thing.

During meditation, as one tries to keep focus and quiet, it's inevitable that intrusive thoughts will start appearing before long. Any obstacle that comes in between you and your self realization could be considered the "Devil."

But don't try to kill this Devil. If intrusive thoughts, emotions, physical sensations, or external hindrances distract you from meditating, simply acknowledge them. You don't have to engage or try to analyze them. Just allow them to pass by like clouds parting to reveal a clear blue sky.

When you have reached a desired level of harmony with the stage of Complete Mind, move on to the next step.

If you meditate and the Devil comes, make the Devil meditate. - Alejandro Jodorowsky (oral transmission via G. I. Gurdjieff)[9]

LOCATION: THE PORTAL
EXERCISE: THE PURIFICATION RITUAL

In ancient times, the Wa'eb priesthood was responsible for the cleanliness and purity of the temple. While visitors today need nothing more than a ticket to enter the temple, for thousands of years, one had to be pure before walking through this portal.

The Egyptian priests would rely on sacred lakes, but since we do not have access to one, a purified bottle of water may be used instead.

But what exactly is "purified" water? The Rosicrucians have a mystical practice for purifying water on one's own which you can carry out during your visit.

WATER PURIFICATION

To proceed with the practice, first take a bottle filled with clean water and hold it level with your solar plexus. Both palms of your hands should be flat on opposite ends of the bottle.

Next, close your eyes, and concentrate on the energy centers that are present in your hands. Inhale deeply and hold your breath for at least three seconds (or for however long is comfortable) before exhaling. This produces an effect on the water in the bottle.

After concentrating in this way for approximately three minutes, slowly drink the water.

According to the Rosicrucians, this practice not only charges the water with the vibrations of one's aura, but it allows the water to become impregnated with the magnetism that continually emanates from our hands.

In this specific case, the energy is predominately positive, producing a magnetization effect which confers the power of regeneration to the water, thus purifying it.

Water is an important part of life to Rosicrucians. We use it in psychic and mystical experiments, and for cleansing both the inner and outer physical body. - H. Spencer Lewis[10]

Before entering the temple, you can pour a little bit of this water onto your hands as a sign of physical purification. The drinking of the water, meanwhile, symbolizes mental purification. But it's also vitally important that you enter the temple with the appropriate intent.

Only after vanquishing the enemy, one may enter the temple. Now you are ready to cross the threshold. The act is done. So mote it be.

LOCATION: THE COURT OF RAMESSES II (THE SHIN)
EXERCISE: INNER FOCUS

As you enter the temple, you'll immediately be able to spot the knee of the striding colossus in the Courtyard of Ramesses II. R.A. Schwaller de Lubicz called this area the Hall of Marchers.

If you'll recall, the statues are depicted with their left foot forward (see p36). You have previously practiced placing your awareness in your feet. Now that you're inside the temple and prepared to take the next step, focus your attention there once again, specifically on the left foot.

Focus on a single toe and imagine each tiny cell vibrating from within. Start to feel the energy fill your entire foot and move slowly up through your left shin and into the knee. Feel the vibration of your left knee.

Now do this exact same exercise with your right foot. Eventually, you will feel both your knees vibrating and tingling.

Your body is full of a myriad of energy currents and this practice helps you to activate them. Don't forget: you are a living, breathing mystery school - a walking Temple of Man.

Bringing this energy up to the knee is comparable to the statue taking its first step. As you proceed deeper into the temple, you will continue to raise this vibration higher and higher.

On that note, it's important to keep in mind the teachings of G.I. Gurdjieff, who emphasized how actually feeling something and just *thinking* you're feeling it are two different things.

In the teachings of Gurdjieff's esoteric school the Fourth Way, the human machine contains three different centers: intellectual (related to logic and the brain), emotional (related to the nervous system and concentrated in the solar plexus), and a moving center (related to rhythm and movement, i.e., "intelligence in motion"). Gurdjieff also emphasized how the three systems must be in balance with one another for a person to attain their spiritual goals.

Similarly, the Temple of Man could also be considered to have multiple interrelated centers (recall the three main axes, for example). Understanding each one and their connection with one another is no easy task, but you are already on your way with these exercises.

LOCATION: THE COLONNADE (THE FEMUR)
EXERCISE: INNER FOCUS

The symbolism of the seven columns and their relation to cycles are explained on p55. In this section of the temple, you are going to continue to raise your vibration through breath and number.

You will begin by taking seven negative breaths, which involves beginning with a complete exhalation. Then, with your lungs empty, hold your breath for as long as comfortable before inhaling deeply.

During the process, your red corpuscles will pick up oxygen from the inhaled air and carry it through the bloodstream to the rest of your body.

Begin by orienting your body beside the first column and extending your left foot forward. Imagine seven segments of equal space from your knee to your waist.

Use the seven columns of the Colonnade as a benchmark. The first column corresponds to the lower region located just above the knee.

For the first breath, bring your attention within and place it on your knee. As you visualize the first of the seven divisions, feel the sublime energy in your left knee.

Finished with the first breath, proceed to breathe naturally in a way that is most comfortable for you. Then start walking to the second column, but don't lose focus on the energy in your knee. And as you take your second negative breath, imagine the energy rising to the next segment of your femur.

Repeat the process with each of the remaining columns. You will feel the energy getting more intense with each negative breath. Visualizing it as an electrical current can be helpful.

This exercise not only helps you raise energy through your body, but it also increases your self-awareness in general.

Having taken the seven negative breaths, one for each column of the Colonnade, imagine that you've animated all the forms required to carry out the divine plan.

You will finish beside the seventh column, where the Opet feast is depicted in relief on the western wall (fig. 41).

We nourish our cells not only through food, but also through the oxygen of each breath. The positive polarity of cosmic energy is received from breathing while the negative polarity of our vital life force is consumed through eating and drinking. Proper breathing will keep our physical and metaphysical bodies in a state of perpetual balance.

You are now ready to enter the Peristyle Court, a section of the temple associated with a myriad of bodily functions and cosmic principles.

LOCATION: THE PERISTYLE COURT
(THE REPRODUCTIVE ORGANS & SOLAR PLEXUS)
EXERCISE: INNER FOCUS

As you pass through the portal into the Peristyle Court, you will first enter the part of the temple associated with reproduction. The next exercise, therefore, relates to the lower root chakra.

As commonly taught in Eastern traditions, the human body contains seven main energy centers known as chakras. Accordingly, Luxor Temple, the Temple of Man, should be thought to have its own chakra system as well.

YONI MUDRA WITH INTONATION OF MAR

In Eastern philosophies such as Hinduism and Buddhism, mudras are ritualistic hand gestures (or sometimes performed with other parts of the body).

One particular mudra known as the *yoni mudra* is said to help awaken one's kundalini energy, calm the nervous system and benefit the reproductive system. Furthermore, using this hand gesture during your meditation will help channel your body's energy flow into your sex organs.

You can also use intonations to more deeply connect to the chakras in your body, your personal temple, as well as to those in the Temple of Man.

Vowel sounds are couriers of specific energies that manifest physically, psychically, and spiritually. These energies affect matter and consciousness, and each vowel sound corresponds to a particular area in your body, healing it on a mental and physical level. Some believe they can even be used to awaken certain dormant psychic faculties.

You are standing at the sacral base of the temple. Sacral refers to the sacrum, or the triangular bone at the base of the

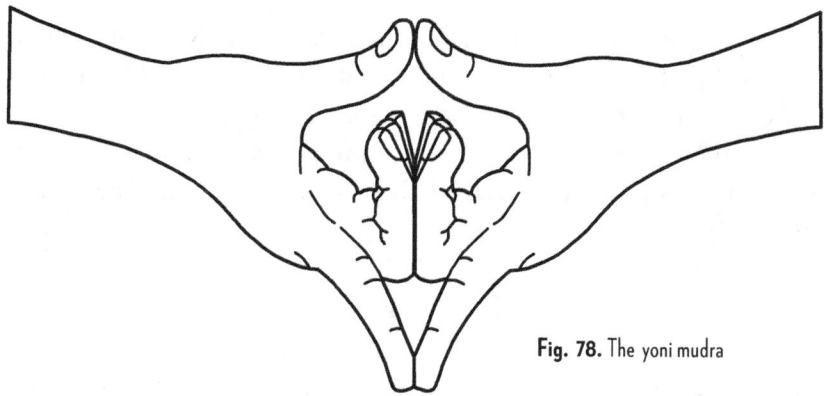

Fig. 78. The yoni mudra

spinal column. (The word originally comes from the Latin *sacer*, meaning sacred.) For this exercise, find a place near the entrance, though you can go off to the side for a bit more privacy.

First, let's form the *yoni mudra*. Connect both of your thumbs and both of your index fingers with one another. With the tips of your index fingers touching, point them downward, creating an upside-down triangle (not unlike the Rosicrucian apron). The backs of your other three fingers on each hand can rest against each other in the middle (fig. 78).

Next, subtly place this triangle over your reproductive region.

This upside-down triangle represents the formless turning into form. The shape is an alchemical symbol for the element of water along with the feminine principle.

Furthermore, this shape resembles a uterus, much like the symbolic head of Hathor, whose face simultaneously resembles a cow and a uterus with two ovaries. Whether you're male or female, the shape also resembles your pelvis.

You can think of applying this mudra as adorning your metaphysical apron as you commence the Great Work.

If you have challenges with fertility or other reproductive health issues, it can be helpful to intone the vowel sound MAR while performing the *yoni mudra*.

First, take a deep breath in and then intone MAR as you exhale. Repeat this three times in accordance with the immutable esoteric law of three, also known as the Law of the Triangle.

If you prefer not to draw attention to yourself, you may quietly intone this sound, which will still produce a similar vibrational effect within.

COSMIC NAVEL MEDITATION

All life begins from the navel, or *omphalos*, and spreads outwardly. While you were in your mother's womb, you were connected to your mother via an umbilical cord coming out of your navel. And the Peristyle Court of Luxor Temple also corresponds to the navel.

As you walk further across the court to this particular point, imagine that you're traveling through the psychic navel, the center of creation. Reaching the area of the navel, find a comfortable location. (Again, off to the side if you prefer.)

Here you can begin your meditation by intoning the vowel sound MEH (pronounced "may") on C natural above middle C. A digital tuning application can help you find the right note. But if you don't have one, making the sound with the appropriate intent will suffice.

MEH is associated with the solar plexus, a place where our cerebrospinal fibers come together. That's why this area is greatly affected by emotions and why we feel things "in the pit of our stomach" when we're uneasy or under stress.

Lock your fingertips together and place the palms of your hands gently over the solar plexus which will bring a calming feeling. This technique can be used in any scenario in which you're nervous or anxious. Now, proceed to take a deep breath in.

As you exhale, intone the vowel sound MEH. Repeat the intonation three times. Follow it with a moment of silence and reflection.

LOCATION: THE HYPOSTYLE HALL (THE LUNGS)
EXERCISE: RHYTHMIC BREATHING

According to the Rosicrucians, life begins when a child takes its first breath and life ends when they take their last. This is the same concept we have explored when discussing our vital life force, the animating principle of all life.

RHYTHMIC BREATHING EXERCISE

As you make your way into the Hypostyle Hall, the section of the temple corresponding to the lungs, it would be appropriate to do some positive breathing.

A positive breath is when you inhale deeply through your nose, holding the breath in your lungs for a certain amount of time before exhaling, also through your nose.

For this exercise, you are going to simulate the rhythmic ebb and flow of waves.

First, visualize yourself sitting by the ocean, watching the waves flowing and crashing gently on the shore. Imagine the inhalation as the flow and the exhalation as the waves crashing upon reaching the shore.

Next, take a deep positive breath in and hold. You can either use a count of seven seconds or simply hold your breath for as long as it is comfortable.

As you exhale, intone the vowel sound KHEI (pronounced "kay-ee") on E natural. This sound is associated with the kidneys and also helps with hormones that regulate metabolism, the immune system and blood pressure, among other things.

After already having intoned the vowel sound KHEI, hold your breath while keeping your lungs empty for seven seconds. Then take another deep breath and intone this sound again until you say it three times in total.

Again, if you prefer, you can also quietly intone or subtly hum the sound with your mouth closed.

By performing positive breaths, we are completing an energetic cycle from negative to positive. Just as negative and positive currents come together to produce electricity, you are charging your physical and metaphysical batteries with these exercises.

Next, you will invoke the principle of Hermes Trismegistus, the Thrice Great.

THRICE GREAT BREATHING PRACTICUM

We as humans have not been taught how to breathe correctly, which is why so many spiritual exercises are centered around proper breath.

Place your hand on your diaphragm and take a deep, slow breath in as you feel your stomach expand. Follow this with a slow expansion of the rib cavity.

Finish with an upper lung expansion of breath so that you can feel the air all the way up into the throat. Then exhale completely, starting at the base of the lungs and finishing at the top of the lungs. Each exhalation should take twice as long as each inhalation.

For example, you can inhale for a count of eight and exhale for a count of sixteen, the exact number of columns on either side of the Hypostyle Hall. If you'll recall, the columns here correspond to the phases of the moon.

Continue concentrating on filling and emptying all three levels of the lungs. When ready, proceed to the next section of the temple.

LOCATION: THE CHAMBER OF DIVINE KINGS (THE HEART) - EXERCISE: RHYTHMIC BREATHING

When you enter the Chamber of Divine Kings, imagine that you are standing in the kingdom of the heart. The heart is renowned by all world cultures as the organ of peace.

Whether you're conscious of it or not, the heart organ produces its own electromagnetic field which can influence the things around it. Learning to be in tune with your heart center will let you tap into this field.

Begin by placing your hand over your heart. Shift your consciousness there. Feel your heart as it beats. You are creating an equilibrium within the body. By feeling and listening to the rhythm of your heart, you will bring yourself into a trance-like state.

Start becoming aware of not only your physical heart but your inner spiritual heart. Focus on the distinction between subtle and gross.

Continue the meditation by intoning the vowel sound EH (pronounced like the letter A) on middle C. Rosicrucians use this vowel sound to help stimulate the psychic center corresponding to the heart.

Take a deep breath and hold it for as long as comfortable. Upon exhalation, intone the vowel sound EH and visualize your heart center as a yellow sphere. Repeat for a total of three times.

Feel the energy radiating in your heart center. Let your heart radiate peace. Remember that all hearts are connected.

Complete the meditation with the Kemetic (ancient Egyptian) yoga pose of Ka.

For more privacy, you may venture off into one of the side chambers associated with the King's royal *ka*. As you take a step forward with your left foot, feel yourself stepping into your power. Raise both your arms, forming a right angle with each arm as your palms face forward.

This is the position of the *ka*, which for the ancient Egyptians was a symbol of divine connection. You are connecting with the divine source, thus completing the cycle initiated by the exercise.

LOCATION: THE OFFERING VESTIBULE (THE THROAT)
EXERCISE: BLOCKAGE REMOVAL

You are now in the section of the temple which corresponds to the throat. And while you are here, you are going to master the Word. The Word is the expression of the creative divine will.

Stand on the point of the intersecting axes, which could be considered a place where the right-hand and the left-hand paths cross (fig. 66).

Cross your arms, left over right, and speak your truth here in the Offering Vestibule. To clear your throat chakra from any metaphysical blockages, say one thing you have not been able to say before out loud. Something you have been holding back or holding inside. Let go of that truth here as an offering to Amun.

Of course, with other people around, you may not want to say it very loudly. Instead, you can whisper it or simply remain silent and think about it. Thoughts have wings.

The Sanskrit word for the fifth chakra is *vishuddha*, which means to purify the body from harmful substances. Let go of the remaining trauma in your body as you release these words. Purify yourself from these stagnant pockets of negative energy that have been living in your body for far too long.

Mystics believe that a blocked throat chakra can cause thyroid disease or any other type of throat ailment. Feel your throat relax as your throat chakra becomes unblocked. You are on your way to becoming a great communicator!

Fig. 79. Vishuddha, the throat chakra

LOCATION: THE HALL OF THEOGAMY (THE THYROID GLAND) - EXERCISE: CONNECTION WITH INNER VIBRATIONS

SACRED VOWEL SOUND INTONATION

Take a deep positive breath in, and hold your breath for as long as it is comfortable. As you exhale, you will intone the vowel sound THO (pronounced with a hard *th*, as in "thought") on F#. Repeat it three times.

The thyroid is regulated by the pituitary gland and helps release the hormones our body needs to discard in order to keep the physical body in balance. The vowel sound THO will assist the thyroid gland.

If you'll recall, this hall that's associated with the throat is also dedicated to the divine birth of the king. Interestingly, Abracadabra in Aramaic is loosely translated as "As you speak, you create."

LOCATION: THE SHRINE OF ALEXANDER (THE MOUTH) EXERCISE: CONNECTION WITH INNER VIBRATIONS

INTONATION: OHM

In the beginning was the Word. (John 1:1)[4]

In the Central Barque Shrine, you'll be intoning the sacred Sanskrit vowel of Ohm. In both Hinduism and Buddhism, it's regarded as the first word, or the primordial sound that created the world. It's from this vibration that all life forms sprang forth.

Form and creation are a result of vibration. Notably, the words Aum, Amen (Amun) and Ohm are almost identical in vibratory rate.

Take a deep positive breath in and hold your breath for as long as it is comfortable. As you exhale, you will intone the vowel sound OM (pronounced simply as Ohm) on D natural. Repeat this three times.

Emphasis should be on extending the *m* at end of your intonation. The extension of *m* will cause a strong vibration within you, allowing you to become one with the sound.

Ohm also is associated with the pineal gland in the middle of our heads, which is believed to be the seat of the soul.

LOCATION: THE HALL OF TWELVE COLUMNS (THE EYES)
EXERCISE: INNER FOCUS VISUALIZATION TECHNIQUE

ALTERNATE NOSTRIL BREATHING METHOD

Close your eyes and go within. Visualize yourself in a state of peace and happiness. Imagine that you've already achieved the goal you chose to focus on at the temple entrance. See yourself living your best life.

Smile outwardly and allow the sense of peace to sink into every cell throughout your body. Forgive yourself for any guilt or trauma that is weighing you down. Remember that love is medicine.

Use your finger to block one nostril, and using the other nostril, rapidly breathe in and out twelve times (one for each column in this hall).

Let go and repeat the technique with the other nostril.

This exercise helps reset the brain's electromagnetic field, bringing the two hemispheres into proper balance. It also helps the nervous system begin healing after letting go of stored trauma.

LOCATION: THE TRIPLE SANCTUARY (THE THIRD EYE)
EXERCISE: CONNECT WITH YOUR INNER VIBRATION

THE RA MA SEQUENCE

The Third eye is often attributed to psychic vision. For the ancient Egyptians, Ra was the solar principle representing fiery red male energy and a positive, active charge.

His daughter Ma'at, meanwhile, represented the feminine and earth element which is of a negative, receptive charge. Ma'at also represented the concept of cosmic harmony.

The Rosicrucians commonly intone the vowel sounds RA and MA together. RA stimulates while MA soothes.

Start this meditation by placing your right index finger toward your pineal gland, the third eye, which is located just above your eyebrows in the center of your head.

Close your eyes and with your eyelids closed, shift your gaze upward and inward toward the apex that is your pineal gland.

Take a deep positive breath in and hold your breath for as long as it is comfortable. As you exhale, intone the vowel sounds RA MA. When intoning RA, keep the emphasis on the *r*. And when intoning Ma, keep the emphasis on the *m*.

Intone each vowel for an equal length of about seven seconds each in order to maintain a balance between the two energies. Repeat the sequence three times.

You have now raised the vibration throughout your entire physical being from toe to head. Take a moment to observe how you feel.

LOCATION: OUTSIDE THE TEMPLE (THE CROWN CHAKRA) EXERCISE: WHITE LIGHT VISUALIZATION

Outside the temple, look for the Ankh that marks the beginning of the central axis, the Axis of Mut (fig. 74). Stand with your body in alignment with it.

Now close your eyes and visualize a large ball of radiant white light a few inches over your head. It should appear as a halo or an aura.

Imagine the sphere of light transiting from above your head and slowly descending through the crown, filling your entire being, from head to toe, with a white hue.

Take a deep positive breath in, and hold your breath for as long as it is comfortable.

As you exhale, you will intone the vowel sound THAW. Repeat it three times to harmonize your entire being.

You have just activated your psychic body. Stay still and feel the energy flowing through you.

Be open and ready to receive any new impressions. You are encouraged to journal whatever you experience in your meditations.

With focus and practice, you will be able to feel the energy and openness in your body. You will become more conscious of the Temple in Man.

Like a rose coming into blossom, each physic center will continue to unfold and open up as you mature in your spiritual development.

It is said that kundalini lies dormant, operating unconsciously until it is awakened. The awakening of your inner kundalini is the true beginning of your journey within.

> It is no wonder that the ancient Egyptians adorned the outer portals of their temples with carvings of serpents weaving up towards heaven, for that was the experience that awaited the initiate within the temple walls. Rapture is the spiritual ecstasy, metaphysical ambrosia, melting in God.[8]

If the reliefs on the walls of the Temple of Man can teach us anything at all, it is that communion between humanity and the divine cosmic principle is possible and attainable within this lifetime.

Know thyself, for you are a living Temple of Man.

NOTES

1. de Lubicz, R. A. S. (1981). Temple in man: sacred architecture and the perfect man. Inner Traditions.
2. West, J. A. (2018). Serpent in the sky: The high wisdom of ancient Egypt. Quest Books.
3. West, J. A. (1995). The traveler's key to ancient Egypt: A guide to the sacred places of ancient Egypt. Quest Books.
4. New International Version. (1984). John 1:1
5. de Lubicz, R. A. S. (1998). The temple of man. Inner Traditions/Bear & Co.
6. Rimbaud, A. (2011). Illuminations. Translated by John Ashbery. W. W. Norton & Company.
7. Star, J. (1997). We can see the truth in your eyes. In Rumi: In the arms of the beloved (p. 123). Penguin Compass.
8. Stratton, H., & Michala, P. (2000). Showing up: An action plan for personal growth and following your bliss. Brown Books Pub. Group.
9. Jodorowsky, A. (oral transmission via G. I. Gurdjieff, date unknown)
10. Lewis, H. S. (1974). The miracle of the water. AMORC.

ABOUT THE AUTHOR

Anyextee is a former music industry CEO, renowned symbolist author, Award-winning filmmaker and one of the world's leading researchers of ancient knowledge, sacred science, and esoteric traditions.

He gained recognition as the producer and voice behind "The Sacred History of the Rosicrucians" and "Ancient Egypt Mystery Schools," in addition to his work as an artist and award-winning documentary filmmaker.

Described as "a firehose of knowledge," Anyextee shares his expertise through lectures across the globe, including significant contributions at the Conference on Precession and Ancient Knowledge. His insights have been featured on the Travel Channel, Rosicrucian TV, and his popular YouTube channel, in addition to various documentaries, podcasts, and radio shows. While writing this book, he resided in Luxor, Egypt, immersing himself in the local culture and history.

Anyextee is also the guiding force behind esoteric tours to some of the world's most sacred locations, including Egypt, Turkey, Mexico, Peru, Bolivia, and Easter Island, through his leadership of Adept Expeditions.

Website: **anyextee.com**
Tours: **adeptexpeditions.com**
Teachings: **ancientegyptmysteryschools.com**